WALKING FAITH FORWARD

WALKING FAITH FORWARD

Perspectives of Ordinary Life Transformed by Faith

Daily events, as seen through the eyes of a woman pursuing a stronger relationship with Christ

Melanie Blievernicht

PUBLISHED BY WESTVIEW, INC., NASHVILLE, TENNESSEE

WALKING FAITH FORWARD
Perspectives of Ordinary Life Transformed by Faith

© 2007, 2010 Melanie Blievernicht

All rights reserved, including the right to reproduction in whole or in part in any form.

ISBN 978-1-935271-49-9

Second edition, May 2010

Printed in the United States of America on acid free paper.

PUBLISHED BY WESTVIEW, INC.
P.O. Box 210183
Nashville, Tennessee 37221
www.publishedbywestview.com

For Jesus, in love and thanksgiving

Contents

Contents vii
Acknowledgments ix
Preface xi
Preface to the Second Edition xiii
Speak It 1
Where Credit Is Due 4
Street Signs for the Soul 6
Theological Incorrectness 8
The I Am 11
Learning to Ask 13
The Right Decisions 16
Casual Promises 19
The "Gotta-Have-It-My-Way" God 21
An Unexpected Lesson in Compassion 24
A Fountain of Patience 27
Where Is He Not? 29
God's Watering Can 31
The Perfect Referee 34
Talking to Our Lord: Meaningful or Mechanical? 37
To Have Faith 41
In His Eyes 43
As Simple as Cause and Effect 45
Quiet the Distractions 49
Panic: The Path away from Christ 51
A Rock-Throwing Society 54
Servanthood: An Inspiration and Dedication to Love 57
No Substitutions, Please 60
The "Closeness-to-God" Game 63
Friendship Revealed 65
Baptism Confusion 67
Overcoming Pain and Disappointment 71
The Master Gourmet 73
The Do, Are, and Will Be 75
Sales Pitch of Satan 78

Men and Fish	81
Faith and Optimism	84
Loneliness	86
Thanksgiving through Trials	89
A Message That Gets Lost in Translation	91
True Confessions	94
His Invisible Touch	96
What Kind of Student Are You?	99
God and Dogs	101
The True Follower	104
Under Attack	106
Jesus, the Universal Language	109
Completely Obedient	111
Moths Don't Know Any Better	113
The Altar of God	115
A Blessing by Choice	118
The Ability to Say No	120
His Timing	122
Christmas Traditions	124
Hypocrite or Not?	129
The Supreme Divider	132
Are You Ready?	134
Observation	137
Afterword	139
References	141
Endnotes	145
About the Author	147

Acknowledgments

I have been overwhelmed by the blessings of people in my life. God has placed an abundance of love and spiritual support in my path, and I would like to express my gratefulness to him and to them for how they have touched my heart and spirit.

I thank my husband who has challenged me in many ways to strengthen my faith and examine my beliefs. His love and passion for the Gospel provide insight and animated conversation as well as enrich our intimate spiritual path as a couple. His encouragement and enthusiasm for my relationship with Jesus has been one of his top priorities, and I feel constantly humbled and amazed that God chose this person for me. I have been given a tremendous gift in his presence in my life. My love, respect, and appreciation for him, both as a Christian and as my husband, have flourished as our faith has grown. I am eager to see what God has in store for our family.

I am grateful to my parents for their never-ending support and for being open and honest about their faith. One of the greatest gifts they have given me was the love, freedom, and lack of criticism when I needed to explore my faith on my own, away from churches, classes, and judgment. They have celebrated my triumphs and struggles equally, always knowing that God uses each to make us who we are. From day one of my marriage and consequent moving away from home, Mom would send me notes, e-mails, and care packages of affection, but hardly any of them closed without mention of my parents' daily prayers for us, for whatever our needs. What a blessing and comfort! To pray with them, experience how they honor Christ, and bear witness to their ministry of others has resounded within my memory for many years. How blessed am I that God saw fit to give them to me!

To my dear friend, Lisa Yezzi: I couldn't have done it without you. Thanks for prompting (hounding) me to write this book of "just thoughts" to share with others. I am so fortunate to have your wisdom and life lessons to provide a sounding board for this work. You amaze me with your perseverance and "walking the talk" in your everyday life. I know that God will continue to bless your faith, love for others, and devotion to your son. I am grateful that God introduced us, since you are a strong Christian woman, mentor, and friend.

Mary O'Donnell, I am forever thankful for your revolving door and eagerness to share God's word. You have been a wonderful cheerleader, and I appreciate the time you put aside to listen to my ideas and compositions. You and your family have been like guardian angels for Bill, the puppies, and me. Jesus knew that this project was on its way and made sure that he provided the necessary resources to see it through to fruition. Thank you for energizing me with your feedback and praying with me in times when Satan tried to cast his doubt upon my mind and heart. You, Dan, and the girls are fantastic examples of how families thrive when their focus is upon the Lord.

So many other people hold special places in my heart and have prayed for me/us during our journey. I thank my family and friends for their support, especially through some challenges we've had these past few years. We have never felt helpless or alone, compliments of your words, cards, and gestures. I send a warm hug out to our spiritual family, who surrounds us with prayers and kindness each day, so that you may know how much we praise God for the faith and strength you have used to lift us up. We feel so blessed in knowing you. Our cup overflows!

Preface

My only qualification for writing *Walking Faith Forward* is that I am a single member among the billions of God's family. My life probably appears average to most, though I feel that it continues to become richer and deeper with each passing day, thanks to Christ's love for and patience with me. I ruminated on ways to introduce people to the text, since I've hardly considered, written, or published anything that has affected me as profoundly as this work. These chapters sprang from my personal experiences across the spectrum of life's adventures, struggles, beliefs, observations, celebrations, pain, and dreams, the common element of which has been the strength and clarity provided by my faith. Although the words flowed easily from my pen, I remain uncertain of the specific purpose of the text. Will it give comfort to the suffering? Direction to the lost? Confidence to the doubtful? I have no idea. I simply felt called to write and share my relationship with Jesus, as if someone out there needed to read these words.

Whatever the purpose may be, I have poured my love, prayer, and hope into *Walking Faith Forward*. If even a single person grows closer to Christ by exploring these pages, I will be thrilled! I have followed each section with a Focus for the Week. My intent is that the reader stretches the amount of time spent examining his or her faith over the period of a week instead of just on a day of worship or during a Bible study. Beyond the Focus for the Week is notation of scriptural references relating to the chapter, for those who enjoy diving into God's word.

In lieu of rambling on about my philosophy or feigned writing expertise, I close with a mission statement of sorts. As is appropriate, it's all about him.

> Mankind's only mission is to
> love wholeheartedly,
> thank daily,
> praise vigorously,
> worship enthusiastically,

humble itself before,
listen to the word of,
find comfort in,
seek the guidance of,
submit gladly to,
model itself after,
ask forgiveness of,
realize its hopelessness without,
dedicate itself to,
read the scriptures of,
release our fears and insecurities to,
share the Gospel of,
glorify passionately,
embrace the commandments and teachings of,
sing joyfully to,
believe the promises of,
trust completely,
draw strength from,
witness miracles of,
have faith in,
serve loyally,
minister to those in need in the name of,
receive grace through,
and be in awe of the generous sacrifice of
Jesus Christ.

Preface to the Second Edition

Back in August of 2007, I published this book for the Lord. Since its release, there have been some significant changes in my life – the most profound of which is divorce. Therefore, the accounts of my life found in the following pages have taken a dramatic shift (see my latest book, *Divorce Is Only Human*). However, this transition does not in any way detract from the spiritual content and truth of what God shared with me during the stage of my life when the events contained herein took place. These observations and reflections are just as relevant to me today as they were when I first sat down to journal them years ago. I hope my experiences will encourage you to strengthen your own relationship with the Lord.

Please note: I have dropped my married name and adopted my maiden name once again. The first edition was published under the name of Melanie Reynolds.

Speak It

Tonight, I stretched out on the sofa and prepared to write. I asked God to send me inspiration, and after a few moments, the telephone rang. Frustrated by the interruption, I picked up the cordless telephone and glanced at the caller ID. The number was local, so I answered. I could immediately tell that the gentleman on the other end of the line was a volunteer for a charitable organization. My mind and stomach flip-flopped, as I realized that we had no money to give due to our financial challenges, and this fact made solicitations awkward. His voice smoothly continued through the prepared speech, and I respectfully waited until he was finished. Feeling inadequate and a little embarrassed, I humbly explained our inability to donate and requested that he forward us whatever donation form he had for the possibility of a future donation.

This sweet man expressed his compassion for our situation, and I told him not to worry, that God had always and will always provide whatever we need. Then it happened. Like a shot of electricity through our veins, we became swept up in conversation about our Lord. He shared his childhood experiences as a preacher's son and the type of example his father had been as a Christian, living God's word in thought, action, and modest lifestyle. My energy went into high gear, as I excitedly related to his faith-filled stories and recounted some of my own. We almost couldn't wait to share our next anecdote and affirmation of God's glory. Praise came from our lips, and somehow a healthy thirty minutes flew by.

When he finally had to go, I regretted the impending hang-up. Before he moved on to the next call on his lengthy list, he genuinely thanked me for openly discussing Christ with him. I expressed the same, since the sharing was so unexpected and so motivating. Jesus' Holy Spirit does that for my soul; it comes into my being in different times and places and comforts, inspires, calms, drives, and creates through me. I suddenly laughed, and I heard his questioning response come over the line. I explained my conundrum about needing a topic about which to write, and my chuckle was for seeing the call for what it really was—God calling with a lead. After we had encouraged and strengthened each other in following our Savior, we finally hung up.

The message to me was clear. God should be a natural part of our daily lives. Speaking his name should not be reserved for the churchgoing crowd or only to be mentioned in politically correct places. We need to speak it; the truth of God should be heard as freely as the weather forecast on television or what you may be having for lunch.

For example, I no longer say that someone is lucky. I used the term *blessed* instead because luck does not exist in the presence of God. Faith is not a gamble. Also, I openly take time to bless my food during meals, even if I am eating with friends or coworkers who may not be Christians. Those who are present often appreciate the opportunity to join in and give thanks, sometimes adding an intention themselves. It should be that simple.

Affirmation of faith can happen in the strangest places, from fast-food restaurant lines to people walking by you on the sidewalk. God never ceases to amaze me in how he uses others in incredible ways to fulfill his will. Though I will probably never be someone who perches on a street corner and proclaims the Holy Gospel, I admire those who do. My greatest excitement has come from unexpected encounters I've had with fellow Christians.

Let us not be reserved in glorifying his presence in our lives. Speak his name. Speak of his Gospels. Speak of his majesty. Speak with love for him. Don't lecture, but share. Don't condemn, but give hope. Don't force, but offer enthusiasm and passion. Don't be self-conscious, but have confidence. Worry not about whom you will offend, since Jesus outranks them all. Let us speak of Christ in the same manner and with the same frequency that he did in honoring us with his life.

I look forward to my next encounter with an unsuspecting fellow believer, and my preconceived notions regarding telephone solicitors will never be the same. How I do love God's surprises!

Focus for the Week

Step outside of your comfort zone and speak to a stranger each day this week. When the opportunity arises, speak of your faith, however short the conversation may be. Let your sharing be genuine, affectionate, and relevant to your conversation, so that those around you will sense your passion for Jesus. You need not include his name in every sentence; your actions and sincerity can extend the message.

Passages

Ephesians 1:1–17
Psalms 34:1–17

Where Credit Is Due

Praise be to Jesus and his Father for everything forever. Their words and actions have given us all that we need to know and follow in order to establish and maintain an intimate relationship with them. However, beware of those who invoke God's name for their own benefit, whether by giving him credit for words not his or by denying him credit for the ones that are. The scripture is an incredible gift in that it documents the historical development of God's covenant with his people. In addition, the text provides an accurate description of circumstance, culture, and conversation by which generations of man can come to know their Father, his Son, and the Holy Spirit.

Yet the vanity- and power-seekers of today's society often quote scripture out of context or with just enough truth to suit their own purposes, whether it be for control of others or for personal glory in other people's eyes. Even Satan's followers have been indoctrinated to throw out brief biblical passages that, when twisted, seem to indicate that acceptance and love for the devil is appropriate. Unfortunately, the lessons they have been taught regarding the perverting of God's words only worsen their chances for possible salvation.

In the Christian arena, some religious organizations have produced their own versions of God's holy book in order to modify the verbiage for various reasons, from making it easier to read to subtly changing specific verses to infer different meanings. Man should be extremely careful in how he chooses to change the original text of the Bible, even in simple translation. When people talk about "the devil" being in the details, we should remember that adjusting biblical content in any way, even with the best of intentions, gives Satan an opportunity to corrupt the interpretation of the text and provide a means by which man may further offend his creator.

The same is true whenever an individual cites a phrase or verse and claims that it is the word of God, just to give the point at hand heavier weight. Then others deny Christ's words to either discredit his authority and wisdom or redirect attention away from his teachings and messages. The bottom line is this—give full credit to the Trinity for its perfection, grace, and generosity. Let nothing that you discuss regarding the Bible be used for any purpose except sharing the Good News, heeding God's warnings and instructions, and inspiring a deeper relationship with Jesus. Christ did not need to manipulate the truth to effectively share his message, and Christians should follow his example.

Focus for the Week

During this week, spend fifteen minutes each day reading God's actual words to his people. Seek out passages with his lessons in the Old Testament and use the New Testament to absorb Christ's words. Focus on these instructions and try to remember one, particular conversation throughout the day—not all of the details, but the specific lesson or commands made by the Lord. By the end of the week, you will have learned or had a refresher of some very valuable wisdom.

Passages

Deuteronomy 18:18–22
Revelation 22:18–19

Street Signs for the Soul

There I sat—again. The newly-paved cut-through on my way to work now housed a small parking lot full of cars and SUVs, waiting to turn left into traffic. I estimated my place in line (ten or twelve from the front), drew in a very deep breath, prayed for patience, and tried to occupy my mind with something productive. Eventually, my gaze fell from the stop sign to the freshly painted lanes on the pavement. I noted that, even in this day and age, people still don't follow directions, whether plainly laid out in front of them or per the fine print in the DMV's rule book. Then I was struck by how this train of thought directly parallels our relationship with our Father and his Son.

For example, how often does God (or a street sign) tell us to yield, and we decide we know better or can work around the instruction? Have you ever taken a U-turn, only to discover that you ended up going in the wrong direction anyway? When your faith becomes stagnant in tough times, are you blocking the intersection so other believers will stay with you instead of making the effort to keep moving and continue growing on their spiritual paths? Do you pass the struggling stragglers, the fledgling followers of Christ, in a "No Passing Zone," leaving them in your wake rather than looking out for their vulnerability and safety? Have you found God's stop signs inconvenient for your schedule and demanded compromises and exceptions to his wisdom? Do you get irritated that your journey with Jesus doesn't feel like the seventy-mile-per-hour highway trip that you desire but may be closer to creeping through the twenty-five-mile-per-hour school zone? When God asks you to be patient and work together to peacefully merge, are you the entitled one who will ignore his directive and speed ahead, only to cut off a fellow driver? Do you consider detour signs in your life to be optional, or do you trust God's judgment for what you need?

My traffic jam time of reflection provided a new perspective by the time I reached the front spot. Instead of becoming increasingly annoyed, I had remained calm and actually felt grateful for the insight I'd discovered in my surroundings. My focus stayed on his will while the cars had crept out into the frenzy of the morning commute. From then on, I pledged to pay extra, special attention to those street signs, in particular the ones that read "Wrong Way," "No Exit," and "No Parking, Fire Lane." Though the street signs direct your car, it's God voice that directs your life—or should. I had to smile. I guess the throngs of people searching for signs from above might be searching from the wrong perspective. It must be exhausting.

Focus for the Week

Let no street sign go unconsidered this week. Ponder each one and see if you can match its message to an aspect relative to your relationship with God. Use these reminders as daily prompts to dedicate ongoing effort and attention to your spiritual growth. Select a specific day and count how many signs helped you to examine your faith.

Passages

Deuteronomy 6:22–25
Matthew 16:1–4

Theological Incorrectness

With each passing day, I become more and more sensitive to Satan's active attempts to shut the Father, Son, and Holy Spirit out of every place—and succeeding on many fronts. For example, people and organizations with no faith have made it their priority to totally eliminate any mention of God's name, whether oral or written, in order to further their own lack of direction or conscience in society. These same individuals surround themselves with people who will not only condone, but also encourage these personal motives, behaviors, and opinions, thereby perpetuating even more anti-God sentiment. They shield themselves from confrontation by using words such as tolerance, diversity, freedom, and rights, but their actions speak volumes to Christians and to Jesus.

Have you noticed that very little is said in opposition to other religions in the United States and around the world? Why is this the case? What is so offensive about Christianity that Satan would spearhead his energy to work against it so diligently? Why hasn't Satan pitted his forces against the Buddhists, Hindus, or Muslims, not to mention the many other religious groups around the world? Perhaps, he behaves this way and through so many channels because he is affirming the one, true God and his almighty Son. It makes perfect and logical sense that Satan only feels threatened by a single being, his creator. There, in itself, lies the answer.

He will do everything he can to hide, discredit, blind, blaspheme, twist, contort, burn, destroy, and manipulate God's words and works to try and win souls to his side. Satan's efforts are the most blatant validation of Christ's presence and future coming. The devil is attempting to make a proportionate response, though whatever he conjures up will always fall short. Therefore, as frustrated as I get with people who are out there spinning their lonely and unfulfilled wheels, their energies give me even more inspiration to openly share and spread God's word. No matter how much they censor, sue, threaten, scream, intimidate, and buy their way into the darkness, they cannot silence the presence of God within us. Christians must continue to keep God's words and teachings upon our lips, in our minds, and within our hearts, though we may be persecuted for doing so. Satan cannot control God's spirit within us, so he will fail to control our faith in God. It is not a relationship into which he has been invited.

From the moment that God cast Satan out of heaven, Satan has been building his army of propaganda to one day challenge his maker. He knows that his time is limited, so he has targeted all of mankind. Already, the world has proved by its actions that Christ gives them a reason to feel threatened, ironic as it seems, since his Gospel, life, and death provided the only true hope for man.

We need to lift up these starving souls in prayer so that God may open their eyes, soften their hearts, and turn their minds toward him and salvation. Evil comes from within a man, and Christ is the only one who can cleanse a person of evil and sin. Our prayers, commitment, and reaching out to these angry, grieving, injured, and lost people would be the least we can do for Satan's followers. They may feel like they have been spiritually abandoned, but we can still ask Jesus to intercede on their behalf. Just as we need to pray daily for God's armor and grace for our fellow Christians, we would be hypocrites to bypass those who suffer without the realization that they are deceived. Jesus, thank you for believing in each one of us, even through your compassionate words to a fellow condemned man as you hung on the cross. Let us demonstrate your love by our determination to pray for the multitudes that would deem our lives and faith not suited for their purposes—just as Christ continued to pray for mankind during his short life. What better testament to his majesty could we offer?

Focus for the Week

The strongest evidence that Jesus is Lord should be seen in how Christians live. Regardless of how many people oppose Jesus and the truth he represents, Christians are responsible for continuing to share Christ's words and life with others. We cannot worry about whom we may offend by our faith. In a day and age when Christians are one of the most persecuted groups on the planet, we need to reach out to those doing the persecuting, whether by prayer or deed. During this week take a few minutes each day to pray for a specific religious group that does not follow our Savior. Direct your prayer and love toward them, that they may come to find him and live with the joy and hope only he can provide.

Passages

Mark 7:14–23
2 Thessalonians 2:8–17

The I Am

You are the soothing calm after a long cry.
You are the lavender in the evening sky.
You are the spring in my step
And the hope in my heart,
You are the sweetness of breath
And the only fresh start.
You are my best friend
An awesome kind ear,
You are the power to mend
And can cast off all fear.
You are my net when I fall
The sacred peace of my soul,
You are the voice, the call
Bringing me to your fold.
You are the breeze on my face
The very depths of the sea,
You are the Creator of stars
And of little ole me.
You are truth for all-time
An eternal light,
You are grace and design
Righteousness and pure might.
You are patience and mercy
Before you I kneel,
You are strength and compassion
And an infant's delightful squeal.
You are loyal to your people
Without waiver or stall,
You are Christ, our Lord Jesus
Who came to save all.
You are perfect in judgment
The single shield against sin,
You remain faithful to us
Though very fickle, we've been.

You are the reason for living
The Lamb, the Lord King,
You are the one for our giving
When we pray, praise, and sing.
You are the miracle of life
The universe and the Earth,
You are saving me a place
That my death brings new birth.
You are the promise that will be.
You are everything to me.
You are.

Focus for the Week

Make a list of images that come to mind when you picture God, his work, and your life. Do certain emotions or feelings pop up? Do certain places come into view? Try to find God's presence in areas of your life where you don't right now. Let his being become part of all of your travel, work, recreation, and home spaces. Enjoy the security and comfort of his Spirit moving with you everywhere you go and let your thoughts dwell on him when you feel idle.

Passage

Exodus 3:13–15

Learning to Ask

Back in grade and high school, I depended primarily on myself to get done what needed to be done. If I wanted to go to college XYZ, then I had only myself to hold accountable for the grades and activities required in order to be accepted. If I desired to buy a particular item, then I had to find the motivation to work odd jobs to provide the income for that purchase. If a night out with friends was my calling, then the house and farm chores needed to be completed beforehand. Primarily, I leaned on my parents for emotional support and providing me with the essentials (supplies, transportation, etc.), but I really didn't want to be too demanding of them for things I could do on my own. It was likewise with my sister. Situations arose where both of us had to work together, but often we preferred divvying up our responsibilities and finishing them at our individual conveniences. So, for most of my life, I have continued to rely heavily upon myself, finding that although I experienced fewer disappointments and frustrations for tasks not getting done, in my independence I also lost the comfort that comes with knowing how to ask for help from those around me.

However, Jesus did not give up on me! Though I am determined to try and handle my life through prayer, personal diligence, and hope, he sees my strong will and stubbornness and knows that I will probably never learn to accept assistance unless it is thrown in front of me, forcing me to concede my inadequacy and inability to cope with everything all of the time. Much of God's reaching out has come from sweet souls I know as family and friends, but his love has also found its way onto my path by way of "Guardian Angel" strangers in passing.

For instance, I was at the local gas station shortly after injuring my back, and I was straining to bend over my engine in order to fill up the oil. The awkward angle was especially painful, but we stubborn folks are determined to do whatever it takes to get things done. Scarcely thirty seconds had passed when a gentleman came rushing out of the convenience store and insisted on taking over the task at hand. I was so grateful I could have cried. Not only did he finish the job, but he also offered to do whatever I needed in the future, if he happened to be there to help. I found out that he was a "usual" at the store, and he was pleased to be available to assist those who couldn't necessarily do for themselves. After showering him with thanks, I drove away, relieved at having had the weight of a simple chore lifted from my shoulders. I immediately praised God for extending His love through that man at a time when I was already struggling with basic, everyday activities.

When I look back at all of the times that Christ has reached out to support and carry Bill and me, I am humbled. From unexpected work that arose during financially trying times to family and friends giving surprise gifts of many kinds, to synchronously-timed telephone calls to see how I was doing, to the spontaneous, generous gestures of strangers, I am in awe. These healing and encouraging situations only reaffirm that God knows better than we what our daily needs will be, and he doesn't have to perform miracles of incredible magnitude when he can use the hearts and spirits of all of his children to help one another. With his tutelage, I am learning to ask for and accept a little more help each day, though it still remains a challenge.

Thank you, Lord, for the people who have given of themselves, with and without my asking, that I may be lifted up in your love. Please let me do the same, in your name, for those who cross my path.

Focus for the Week

If God intended for us to do everything on our own, we would all live on separate planets. He intended for us to look after one another, which requires us to try and excel in giving, but it also demands that we learn how to be gracious receivers. We are not superhuman, so we must acknowledge that asking for and accepting help are essential to our healthy existence. This means that pride and guilt must be put aside and thanks and praise for his grace must be put at the forefront. We ask Jesus for his assistance on a regular basis, so why do we find difficulty in accepting generosity and compassion from our neighbors (whom Jesus probably sent)? This week, take time to examine aspects of your life that could use some outside support. Decide if there is someone who might be able to assist you with a part of your life. In addition, look around you for someone who might need your help. The size of the tasks is of no consequence. The important thing is that you are taking a load off of your own shoulders and reaching out to someone else who needs to be doing the same thing. You need never carry weights that are too heavy for you, since God is ready to lift them for you, even though you may feel alone.

Passage

1 John 3:22–24
Psalms 121

The Right Decisions

The clock read 11:30 PM on a Sunday night. My heart was still racing from the drive to the emergency veterinary clinic with our sweet Ana. Bill had awakened me at 10:00 PM with worries of Ana's sudden drooling, and we practically flew out of the house when we realized her pulse was over 170 beats per minute. Now the vet was entering the room with an X-ray in hand and a solemn countenance. My frantic heart fell into my stomach. She slowly and quietly described the state of Ana's abdomen, in particular her stomach, which was bloated, twisted, and folded back on itself. I remember the words "heart failure," "lack of oxygen," "sedated for now," and "requires immediate surgery to save her life," somewhere through the tears and feeling of dread.

The doctor left us to decide what our wishes would be for Ana. I collapsed onto the nearby bench and tried to silence the hysteria I felt welling up inside me. The sterile and fluorescent-lit room seemed to close in on me. Bill was working through the news by pacing the room, fighting back tears, and absorbing his own shock, fears, and the bite of reality. At heart, we both are the do-whatever-it-takes kind of people when it comes to our babies (our only children, for now). Ana was our first Rottie rescue at two years old, and her old soul is the most gentle and loving of any dog either of us has ever owned. However, the decision was not so easy to make, considering the physical challenges Ana had developed over the last several years. Her hip dysplasia had worsened tremendously, to the point that one hip was "severe" and the other was "moderate to severe." She was not a candidate for surgery due to the seven fused vertebrae in her spine. Both of these conditions made simple tasks such as getting up and down, walking, and going to the bathroom more difficult for her without our assistance. She also knuckled her front feet over when she walked due to her nerve damage, so we had purchased little boots for her to wear to protect her paws. We had done everything we can to keep her quality of life at a healthy level, including supplements, medication for discomfort, an exercise program, special diet, and aqua therapy (thanks to some loving family members who donated enough money for some sessions). Though still a "wobbler" at eight and a half years of age, her spirit and zest for life are spunky and vibrant. She seems comfortable and content.

So, as Bill and I struggled with our decision, I found it difficult to figure out if and how our little girl would recover from a major operation considering all of her other challenges. To compound our devastation, the vet tech returned with the estimate for the surgery. Even the offer of a credit card application did not soften the blow. Alone, again, we were both silent. We clasped hands and made our final decision. We prayed and told Christ that we would not let money be the pivotal factor in Ana's life with us. We told him that we had provided the best life for her that we could, and we would give the go-ahead for the surgery—had she been dying of cancer that would have been a different story altogether. However, we wanted him to decide. We humbled ourselves before his feet and asked that he prepare us for letting her go. We would accept his will and do our best to cope with the outcome, but we asked him to be merciful and take her during the surgery, if it was her time. As long as we knew that whatever Christ chose could only be perfect, we felt confident that the outcome reflected the right decision—honoring the fact that it was not ours to make.

The operation ran from 1:00 AM to 3:00 AM, and they were two of the longest hours of my life. Ana pulled through with flying colors, and she left the vet in record time, arriving home only sixteen hours after her operation.

We revel in every additional moment we have with her, from cute "looks" on her part to silliness on our parts. We praise God for his blessing on her surgery, the vet and techs, our guardian angel neighbors who have watched over us with love, and our lives for the comfort he provides. Sometimes, the situations that teach us the most are the ones in which we stand to suffer the most. We need to honor Jesus in all of our decisions, instead of on an emergency-only basis.

We firmly believe that the tender touch of an angel directed Bill's gaze to Ana and her drooling. He could have very easily been dozing on the couch, upstairs in the shower, or busy in the den on the computer. God provided us with an opportunity to help Ana in a window of time that was very small. Had her distress occurred an hour or so later, she would have slowly died, alone in the dark, only to be found by us the next morning. We are grateful for his allowing us the chance to participate in Ana's life through yet another stage. Regardless of the outcome, we would have accepted his decision with loyal hearts.

Focus for the Week

No matter how uneventful or crazy your week may be, focus on asking God for his guidance with your decisions. Seeking God's hand in important choices should be as routine as saying a blessing, doing the laundry, or calling a friend. Even if you make a poor choice, you can never go wrong asking for the Lord's help.

Passages

Proverbs 3:5–7
Psalms 31:1–3, 9–10, 14, 19, 21, 23–24

Casual Promises

I believe, if my recollection serves me correctly, that there was a time many years ago when most people did what they said they were going to do. They told someone that they would do, be, acquire, or handle something, and so they did. As generations have passed, these people seem to have dwindled. Due to the decrease in follow-through with personal and professional commitments, individuals began to attach phrases such as "you have my word" to emphasize the importance of their verbal commitment. "I promise" became another common suffix to sentences, which then spun out into all sorts of variations. Eventually, in order to out-do the simple promise, people began reiterating their pledges with consequences. For example, "I promise you that I will be there on time. If not, dinner's on me." Does a friend or acquaintance really need convincing through the speaker's self-punishment that the speaker is being sincere?

Obviously, if agreements or promises between two people have reached this point, we have become quite the lying population. Now don't get me wrong; everyone knows that emergencies and unexpected events happen that prevent all of us from being on time or whatever else the case may be. I am more interested in the casual promises that we make to each other that we *know* may not come to fruition. As Christ states in the Garden of Gethsemane, "The mind is willing, but the flesh is weak."

We are an easily distracted society, and we are in the habit of making excuses when our "word" fails to be fulfilled. The commitments we make, regardless of impact or degree, should be taken seriously, for our follow-through, or lack thereof, determines to what degree we are hypocrites (in one respect). A Bible study facilitator once told my class that one way we can avoid letting others down with empty promises is to promise our best effort in trying to complete our task. He laughed and spoke of Paul, who tried over and over again to visit the Christians in Rome. However, God had other plans for him. So, when Paul wrote letters to them from various countries and even from a jail cell, he reassured them that he was still trying his best to get to Rome to share the teachings of Christ with them in person. Though he was waylaid many times, he did not falsely promise that which he knew was out of his control. Most importantly, he truly lived up to his words in that he *did* give the trip his strongest effort. Jesus considers our words and our intent when we commit to others. He knows our hearts and how we plan to act (or not act) on our promises. There are no excuses for lacking the motivation or time to do what you said you would. Be ready and make time.

The only man who fulfilled all that he ever promised is Christ. The actual fruition of his promises may not be witnessed or experienced in this moment, but a day will come when we will revel in every promise that came from his lips. God's living covenant with mankind will be seen through the return of his Son. We will immediately recognize a promise of pure love, with regard only for the well-being of another, without hesitation, and in the time promised. Our day-to-day commitments are quite small compared to Christ's generosity and purpose, but we can still use his life as a guide for our own words. Let me break the habit of casual promises, Lord. Please help me to live with much dedication, intent, and effort behind each of my pledges to others.

Focus for the Week

Try to eliminate casual promises from your dialogue with others this week. Put effort into diligently following through with responsibilities for which you have volunteered or to which you have committed. Do not shirk them due to laziness or poor time management. Make them as high a priority as you would expect others to do, if they were the ones responsible for the tasks instead. Ask your Lord to assist you in staying the course. Let others come to know your words of commitment to be truth, needing no additional emphasis in order to be believed.

Passages

Ecclesiastes 5:2–5
Galatians 3:16–29
Joshua 23:5–11

The "Gotta-Have-It-My-Way" God

When I talk to people who claim not to believe in God, their reasoning often draws the same conclusion; they didn't get what they wanted, when they wanted, and how they wanted, when they chose to give God a chance in their lives.

Children behave similarly with their parents or guardians when they pass an appealing display or product at the store. If the parent does not immediately comply with the child's request for the treat or toy, the request may become a demand, with the threat of a tantrum. If the tantrum fails to yield the desired response, a child may choose to totally ignore the offending parent by pouting and being obstinate, including refusing to engage in future conversations or activities at home. Though displeasing to the child, the process of parents establishing and enforcing boundaries demonstrates that the parents are looking out for the child with total love, concern, discipline and moderation. Children may get frustrated with their lack of control and freedom during this time, but they hopefully will come to trust, respect, and understand the system and how its methodology is actually beneficial for improving their health, safety, respect for others, and ability to make wise choices.

With God the same rules apply, except that we don't stand eye to eye with him each day. There is no bargaining for good behavior or threatening with tantrums. God's perfect wisdom knows exactly what is best for us while we are here. These standards may not be the ones we had in mind for ourselves, but we must trust in him, as our Father, to care for us just as we, as helpless infants resting our confidence in our Earthly parents. He may even surprise us with a better answer to our prayer than we could have imagined on our own.

Contradictory to our illusions of control, we remain helpless without God's guidance. Our misperceptions keep us distant from his voice and direction. Unfortunately, some of God's children will choose to ignore him when his schedule and actions fail to give them the immediate gratification they crave.

These individuals are uncomfortable in giving up their illusions of power to the greater authority. Completely trusting in God takes an incredible amount of effort and will power—letting go of your plans to honor his, not panicking over whether the money you earn will be enough to pay the bills, releasing your loved ones into his care when they are struggling, sick, suffering, or dying, focusing on following his Ten Commandments and lessons as diligently as you can, and shifting your priorities away from the material and toward the spiritual. The tasks are enough to exhaust anyone! Faith in God requires a significant amount of fortitude.

The key to the journey is accepting that God's manner of answering our prayers is flawless in every way. The answer may be contrary to our liking, but we must trust and be grateful that our Father has our best interests in mind. If our lives were easy, always pleasing, full of indulgence, and free of pain, God's presence would not be our main focus. However, suffering and hard times provide windows in our lives when God is forging us in his fire, strengthening us for the future, pulling us into his arms, and reassuring us that all will be well.

So, when life becomes stressful and difficult, step back and see if you're on God's path or your own. Perhaps, he is giving you a nudge or a shove toward a better destination.

Focus for the Week

List times in your life when you expected God's presence to be with you. This list should include times gone by as well as present and future events, including visions of your goals and dreams. Be as specific as you can. Once you have finished, go back to the list and label each item "N" for need or "W" for want. Needs are things that you feel are necessary for your everyday life. Wants are optional things you desire. When finished, ponder this idea: As long and detailed as your list is, God has an even longer one with all sorts of items you didn't even consider. Not only that, but his list also runs from before your conception to your death to your time with him in his eternal kingdom. In addition, he decides which of your Ns or Ws are truly necessary to his plan for you and fills them accordingly. He is not limited to caring for us using the scenarios we create in our minds. He has limitless power and resources by which to provide for us in ways he sees fit. God's wonder and majesty are as constant as they were thousands of years ago, so believe in him or leave him. We don't get a menu from which to choose or judge his leadership abilities.

Passages

Proverbs 3:5–23
Psalms 40:1–17

An Unexpected Lesson in Compassion

My third home, aside from my house and work, is my local grocery store. On one of my daily trips, I fell in behind a car that eased into the prime parking spot up front, so I settled for another spot several rows down. The other driver and I seemed to merge as we neared the front door, and I jokingly commented, "You must be living right to get the top parking spot!" I couldn't make out his mumbled response, as his head was turned away from me, so I continued with, "How lucky was that?" At this, he turned to glance at me from under his baseball cap, and I was shocked by what I saw. Doing my best to control my reaction, I casually noted the brutal scars on the left half of his face, some of them disfiguring his nose, jawline, and mouth, but I kept my gaze directed at him. My mind began searching through possible causes of his scars, from accidents to wartime injuries. He responded, "Well, I don't feel so lucky. Most people turn and run the other way when they see me coming."

We were both still walking, having entered the lobby area of the store, and after finishing his comment, he accelerated away from me through the inner sliding doors and veered left in front of the line of cashiers. At the moment I lost sight of him, time seemed to stop, and all noises were silenced. I stood, rooted to that spot, almost dumbfounded by his words, when I heard three more. From over my right shoulder, only inches from my ear, a man's voice gently spoke, "And Jesus wept." I glanced quickly over my shoulder, but there was no one else in the lobby. Instantaneously, I was aware of a horrible, crushing pain in my chest, as if someone was sitting on top of my heart. I found I couldn't breathe and had started to cry. By the time my hurried steps had taken me to the bathroom inside the store, I was sobbing hysterically and almost hyperventilating. I positioned myself against the wall just behind the bathroom door. I couldn't get control of myself. It was as if someone had opened the floodgates for a lifetime of pain and grief, and I had no way to stop it.

I thought that one of the cashiers might pursue me into the restroom out of concern, since I am a regular customer. But no one did, and I was grateful. Through my sobs I heard a toilet flush and the consequent washing of hands. No closer to regaining my composure, I began to pray that God would blind my presence from whoever was in the bathroom with me. I was having the most overwhelming breakdown of my life, and I didn't want anyone to ask me about it, offer advice, try to empathize, or require any details. What happened next completely astonished me. Though my breaths and muffled cries continued in a jerky and irregular fashion, the girl in the bathroom walked by me without even blinking. All I kept thinking was "don't see me. Don't see me. Don't see me." She didn't. Now you're probably thinking that she was just being polite, but I assure you that even the most socially distant of individuals would have demonstrated some sort of concern for a woman who was behaving as if she had been mugged or injured. She never even glanced in my direction. I'm also certain that she didn't hear me. I was like paint on the wall. Not only did she leave, but also no one else entered until after I left several minutes later.

In total, I had been in the bathroom for about five minutes. Once my cries ceased and my breathing slowed, the calm that settled over me was profound. I immediately had the desire to find this man and tell him that I cared about him. On a mission to track him down in the store, I expediently approached the six or seven cashiers and baggers. I asked them to point me in his direction, since it was obviously a slow time of day. I gave them a general description of his attire and dramatic facial features. They appeared confused and said that they hadn't seen anyone like the person I described. I found this odd since they were just standing around talking when he and I had entered the store. Determined, I hurried over to the service desk, knowing that he had to have passed the counter, but the two attendants gave me the same response. I searched the entire store, talked to people I knew in different departments, and even questioned shoppers. No one had seen him. I finally realized that maybe he had been there for me, just as the words had been. I left the store without any of the items on my list since they no longer seemed important.

The next day I found out that the passage "Jesus wept" is the shortest verse in the Bible. I have only recounted this experience to a handful of family members and friends. No matter how much time passes, whenever I retell the story, my chest begins to hurt, and the tears flow. I cannot assume to know the lesson, but perhaps God was trying to teach me the difference between saying I feel compassion for others and knowing that I do. I will tell you this—if the pain, chest pressure, and tears that overtook me in those few moments were anything like what Jesus felt for his people's pain and suffering, I am in awe of his strength and compassion.

Please, Lord, help me to share your love, mercy, and compassion with those who think I would rather turn away and pick a different path. Help me to live your word and honor my tears, just as you honored yours long ago.

Focus for the Week

Find a way to reach out to someone with compassion this week. Seek out a person who is struggling in some part of his life, someone who has a need that is difficult to resolve on his own. Let Christ's love move through you to that person, that he may feel the warmth and tenderness of God's compassion. It might be through a gift, comforting words, a chore done out of love, or some other simple gesture. Remember that some of Jesus' greatest demonstrations of compassion used the most basic actions and gentle tones.

Passages

2 Chronicles 36:11–16
Exodus 2:5–10
John 11:35

A Fountain of Patience

When discussing Jesus' life with my peers, I find that they often bring up the amazing miracles he performed. These demonstrations were truly phenomenal and laid the foundation of his purpose for coming and sharing his love and the Good News. However, I am also impressed by one of his character traits that is routinely passed over for the more dramatic feats—his constant patience.

Everywhere he went, people demanded his attention, words, guidance, touch, teachings, comfort, and promise of hope. His disciples had daily questions and a consistent desire to learn from him. The common people longed to hear Christ's words of wisdom and see him as he traveled. They grabbed at his person and garments in passing, asking for his mercy and blessings. The Pharisees challenged and antagonized him, trying to entangle him in his own speeches and logic. Even those closest to him had doubts and required reassurance from his lips.

Now imagine that you were in Jesus' shoes. Your sole purpose in each day was to glorify the Father and give, give, give! I can't imagine that Christ had much time for himself during those times. Had he lived in modern times, he would have required quite a massive security detail in order to get through an average day with the public crying "me, me, me" and "more, more, more," without being satiated. The key to his handling such overwhelming circumstances was through the patience he had for mankind. He identified man's shortcomings, pain, fears, questions, confusion, and emptiness and acted with compassion instead of irritation, with love instead of tolerance. If we could only reframe the demands put on us by others in the same fashion, our words might be gentler, our actions more generous, and our hearts more tender.

I think our main hurdle in finding that type of place within ourselves is our selfish nature. Christ's only purpose for anything on any day was to provide for us. Contrarily, we live very self-centered lives that easily block out our availability to and patience for each other. We lack focus and discipline in our interactions with our fellow man because our priorities are concentrated on external things. Jesus had no other goal, concern, or achievement on his mind. Saving us from eternal suffering was his only priority.

Blessed are we that our God put all things in the world secondary to his people, as immature and imperfect as we are. May we strive to extend God's love through our patience to everyone we meet, no matter how stressful they may be.

Focus for the Week

Do you have a short "fuse"? Why? What sets you off the most? Over the next week, if you feel your patience being tested, take a moment to step back and simply wait. Keep those teeth from grinding, the hands from clenching, and the blood pressure from rising. Instead, release whatever importance you placed on that conversation or situation for the time being. This might require remaining silent, pulling your car off of the road, closing your eyes, taking a few deep breaths, or changing the subject. You do not always have to be right, first, or perfect. Somehow, in all of his wisdom, Jesus found direct, calm, and loving ways to address the people around him, even those who probably would have driven an average man crazy. Though we are infinitely far from his majesty, we can still ask him to assist us in finding the patience and respect that he extended to others. When you are releasing a situation, take that moment to ask God for his help in how to respond (or not). Seek his wisdom and grace versus counting on your own witty or sarcastic remarks. Open yourself up, that the Lord may use you as a vessel to demonstrate his patience.

Passages

James 5:7–11
1 Thessalonians 5:14

Where Is He Not?

When people ask "where is God" I say, "Where is he not?" Depending on whom you ask, God is found in any number of places, from a church sanctuary to the local park, to a special place or private room. Although we may feel closer to him in certain places or at specific times, he surrounds us our entire lives.

To put this in a single frame of perspective, consider this: From the bed on which you sleep to the clothes that you wear, to the food you eat and refreshment you drink, to the roof above your head, to the car, bike, truck, or hot wheels that you drive, to the computer on which you work, to the money for which you labor, to the light that wakes you, to the darkness that sees you to sleep, to the roads and buildings along your path, to the wind that sings through the trees, to the life of each rainbow, infant, leaf, bug, blade of grass, star, planet, animal, vegetable, feeling, thought, idea, expression, and freckle, do we not experience God?

His being is in every breath we take, every hug we share, and every possible tangible and intangible thing found in our universe. He was with us in spirit from before we took physical form. He embraces us every moment of each day. No greater love exists. All that he created demonstrates his eagerness for us to be happy. Though he already gave us everything we could need, he willingly gave us a way to return to him through his son. Our relationship became complete when Jesus lived among us, as proof that God understands our pain and suffering and desires to show us his unconditional love. Christ connects heaven and Earth.

God continues to radiate with his passion and affection for us in each new day's miracles and wonders. He is not hidden away in a secret location or through an exclusive group; he is available to us at all times, for as long as we need him, whatever the reason. He will remain steadfast to his children, whether we seek him out or not.

Focus for the Week

Pick three places that you frequent during the day. They could range from your kitchen sink to your desk at work. Sometime this week, identify a person, place, or thing in that area that you don't normally associate with God. It could be living or inanimate, but from now on, let it be a reminder of God's love and desire for you to be happy. From time to time, change these items until you have exhausted those areas. Then pick new ones. Even the dullest of supplies, objects, or buildings had to come from materials provided by God. Your ideas, the weather, and possessions also come from his love. You don't have to look to the heavens to find his fondness and affection for us.

Passages

John 15:9–13
Psalms 24:1–2

God's Watering Can

Tonight, I sat down at the kitchen table to open myself up to God and see if he had anything for me to write. As I prayed for inspiration, I was greeted by a wave of rolling thunder (or as my parents used to say "the potato wagon rolling across the sky"), and the clouds darkened. I knew that this storm would hopefully bring the answer to so many prayers for rain and cooler temperatures through these horrendously stifling days of late summer. I didn't feel seized by any particular topic, so I sat and gazed out the bay window, watching and listening to the progress of the storm.

Our backyard trees, towering overhead, stood quite still through the preliminary flashes of lightning. The two hummingbirds at our feeder decided to move to higher and safer locales. I quietly bid them farewell and the hope of finding a resting place. The winds grew stronger, and surprisingly they seemed to be coming downward instead of across and through my yard. Their gusts thrashed every branch and leaf in sight. Those grand oaks and poplars appeared so stout a moment ago, before the wind rocked, twisted, and battered them into submission.

I am reminded of many things as I sit in awe of the storm. I, once again, recall how small a place I have in the world. My mind enjoys the thrumming of the rain, and the sound takes me back to nights of camping in my family's pop-up, playing cards on rainy evenings, and falling asleep to the millions of droplets on the canvas. Part of me sighs for the trees, plants, and the earth, as the cool sheets of water coat and sooth their dry roots and parched bodies. Often, I will stand in a newly-begun shower in order to experience the cleansing sensation of fresh rain—its fragrance, the chill and smoothness of it on my skin, and its blatant disregard for my presence. Grateful memories of powerful winds and rain spring to mind, since I can still see the yellow blankets of pollen from spring and summer consuming every ounce of air and resting on every surface. My prayers during those nights regularly begged for the mercy of a thorough storm to ease the suffering of people with breathing problems, including my husband with his allergies.

Yet without that pollination, we would be deprived of the very same plant life upon which we rely and most take for granted.

The storm gradually started creeping away, though its voice continued to shake my home periodically. A gentle breeze began coaxing the beaten leaves back to playful lives. A soaked hummingbird braved the onset of darkness for a few final sips at the feeder. Drops of water continued to pitter-pat in various places, creating a repertoire of tiny, resonating voices. I sat in awe of this simple event and how I have experienced its passing. Instead of my usual philosophy of busying myself with chores during a storm, I acquired a much deeper appreciation of this everyday phenomenon. I realized that God's love for me expands beyond my perception of his affection, even to his care of nature, vigorous but sustaining, rough but necessary.

The miracle of storms will always hold my attention, and God's creation of every detail is inspirational. If I sat here long enough, I seriously doubt that I could find even one, imperfect, naturally occurring plant, animal, mineral, or element under heaven. No surprise there, when you consider the designer.

The constant hum of the shower is waning, so I am off to revel in the remnants of God's watering can. My feet are already bare, and my clothes are due for a washing anyway. I will tuck the glorious memory of this storm away and retrieve it during a scorching summer day to come. Thanks, God, for slowing me down enough to really watch you in action in your garden. Before I go, I make a note to myself. Just how many of these fascinating events am I missing? Let me work on paying better attention in the future. Seek them out each day. Now my writing is done, and play is at hand. Hope none of the neighbors are watching!

Focus for the Week

Take fifteen minutes this week to sit and watch an everyday miracle of God. Make the time quiet, not interrupted by the telephone, television, computers, or people. Reflect on what unique part of our creator went into that miracle. Make an ongoing effort to observe and appreciate the magnificent details we often overlook in our busy lives.

Passage

Genesis 1 and 2

The Perfect Referee

Everyone has pet peeves. Generally, they are things that go beyond annoying an individual to the point of setting off an inner barometer that deems the action as unfair, discourteous, or flat-out wrong. For instance, one of my long-standing pet peeves is people who park in handicap spaces but who aren't handicapped. I'm sure that laziness, poor weather, and a self-entitled attitude might all be factors contributing to these squatters' actions. However, I am certain that they are lacking concern for how their behavior prevents those people with physical limitations and challenges from accessing handicap parking spots. During the past few years, I have become particularly sensitive to parking lot predators, since my ninety-year-old grandma cannot go out in public without her walker, a handicap ramp, and an unlimited amount of time with which to move from here to there. Our family has come to rely on these valuable and necessary spaces to ensure her ongoing participation in public, family activities.

My purpose in using this example is not to condemn the people using these spaces without authority. I call attention to it in order to illustrate one of many, everyday events that set off my personal barometer—from people being treated unfairly to those who abuse the rules, to the criminals who rape, pillage, kidnap, and murder, to the exploiters of you-name-it, to those who focus on destroying faith instead of strengthening our God-given opportunities to love and heal, to those who thrive on the misery of others. My list goes on in my mind, but I shall end it there, for now. Simply, I am frustrated by the common thread—the lack of true *justice*.

This is where Christ, the perfect referee, lifts me up and gives me hope. Although I know that almost all of the steps I can take to be fair and just to others are minimal, I can rest assured that his judgment is coming. He will be the true bringer of justice. His justice will not be a sentence subject to be manipulated by lawyers, courts, or the media. His instantaneous, righteous judgment will be swift and without negotiation. There will be no bribes, special cases, excuses, or privileges based on any trait you posses, who you know, or how much you think you know. Each man will answer for every thought, word, and deed in his entire life, each instant examined without bias by the Savior. I, myself, am very intimidated by his coming, and I will have an endless list of items that will be placed before me and for which I will be found lacking. However, I am willing to accept his judgment of my sins, knowing that I am constantly struggling to improve my faith, mind, body, and spirit through Jesus' help.

The knowledge that Jesus will take care of delivering justice to everyone allows me to let go of those instances that set off my barometer with a simple phrase: "God is watching." These three, little words remind me that, though some of man's attempts at facilitating justice are feeble compared to God's, the sentences that he will hand down will be righteous and fair, regardless of the crime. Peace will eventually reign in this world, but its presence will only be felt after Christ has dealt with everyone on an individual basis.

So, the next time you witness an act that seems to violate your inner sense of right and wrong, just remember that God has already made a note of it. Do what you can to right the wrong, but trust that he will be following behind you, in love and righteousness, to truly set things straight, once and forever.

Focus for the Week

What are your pet peeves? Do you ever feel like dealing with the offender yourself? Have you? Were there times when you became upset and could do nothing? When? If these situations occur in the future, offer your frustration and need for justice up to God. Vent your anger and hostility to his attentive ear and ask him to help you move past the sinful thoughts and desires you may have. God has already told us that vengeance will be for him to take, in his time, not in the moment when we want our own justice served. Instead of resentment and negative thoughts for those who violate your standards of appropriate behavior, choose to pray for them. Pray that they could come to see the error of their ways.

Pray that God will move in their hearts and help them to change, so they will have fewer sins for which to answer one day, even if those sins seem small compared to many. Though our fellow man can find numerous behaviors that annoy and irritate us, Christians should always try to handle these trying times in his way, before our own. This philosophy is extremely challenging to practice, but then faith has never been easy.

Passages

Genesis 19:1–29
2 Timothy 4:1–8

Talking to Our Lord: Meaningful or Mechanical?

The Lord's Prayer is a common prayer for Christians. However, we need to remember the entire context in which Jesus shared these words.

> Matthew 6:5–9
> And when thou prayest, thou shalt not be as the hypocrites are: for they love to pray standing in the synagogues and in the corners of the streets, that they may be seen of men. Verily I say unto you, They have their reward. But thou, when thou prayest, enter into thy closet, and when thou hast shut thy door, pray to thy Father which is in secret; and thy Father which seeth in secret shall reward thee openly.
>
> But when ye pray, ***use not vain repetitions***, as the heathen do: for they think that they shall be heard for much speaking. Be not ye therefore like unto them: for your Father knoweth what things ye have need of, before you ask him. ***After this manner*** therefore pray ye:

Our Father which art in heaven, Hallowed be thy name.
Thy kingdom come. Thy will be done in earth, as it is in heaven.
Give us this day our daily bread.
And forgive us our debts, as we forgive our debtors.
And lead us not into temptation, but deliver us from evil.
For thine is the kingdom, and the power, and the glory, for ever.
Amen.

I believe that Christ is sharing with his disciples the *way* to pray, not the specific words to pray.

In the first passage, he denounces those who make a grand demonstration of their praying, since they are seeking attention for themselves instead of genuinely focusing it on Jesus. Jesus prefers our private prayers behind closed doors instead of those made for an audience.

    I also believe that his gift of the Lord's Prayer was to assist those who had no idea where to begin their prayers—not as a dictate to be recited. Why would our Lord specifically teach his followers to avoid repetitions and then contradict himself by asking them to repeat a prayer? He wouldn't. His guidance speaks more to the content of prayer than to its actual verbiage. Some of these points might include speaking directly to our Father, honoring his holiness, acknowledging that he is in total control of all of his creations, asking for his help with our daily challenges, thanking him for our ongoing blessings, asking forgiveness for our sins and shortcomings in the same way he has asked us to treat each other, asking for strength to avoid sinning, and believing that he is all things and deserves all praise and glory for those things.

    Everyone has their own perspective; the important thing to remember is that this prayer was Jesus' way of offering assistance to those who did not know how to pray versus it being a mandate for all men to use to speak to his Father. Jesus, himself, never repeated a prayer, whether a blessing over a meal or words that healed the sick and lame. Why would he ask us to pray any differently?

    Imagine, for a moment, a routine day in your home when you were a child. Now within that day, remember seeing your parents or siblings right after you woke up. Recall your interactions in the morning, during the day, and maybe at the dinner table. Were there any special events that day? Did you leave your home to go out during the afternoon? What did you say to your family as you left? Later in the evening, did you have a routine for heading off to bed? Did you speak to your family members in a particular way? Was there affection shared (hugs, kisses, etc.) with those people who loved you?

    I know that, for me, my parents have always been affectionate. Kisses goodnight, hugs before leaving the house, a shoulder to cry on, and soft words to ease the pain of my sensitive soul were often forthcoming in my home. Hopefully, you can relate to this type of relationship, whether it is with a family member or a friend.

For this example, I will be focusing on my dad, so in your mind, think of your own father or a person who might be like a father figure for you. Don't worry if your person is your mother or another woman who cared for you. The point will be the same. Imagine that, instead of my casual words, hugs, and affection for him, I greeted him the same way every time we spoke. In addition, visualize how that would probably affect him. For instance (in the afternoon), "Hi, Dad" (brief hug). "How are you? I had an okay day at school. My math test was extremely difficult. I will mow the yard this Saturday. Thanks for taking me to the movies over the weekend. Love you." Now (in the evening), "Hi, Dad" (brief hug). "How are you? I had an okay day at school. My math test was extremely difficult. I will mow the yard this Saturday. Thanks for taking me to the movies over the weekend. Love you." Now (before bed), "Hi, Dad" (brief hug). "How are you? I had an okay day at school. My math test was extremely difficult. I will mow the yard this Saturday. Thanks for taking me to the movies over the weekend. Love you." Not only would my repetition probably be boring for him, but he might also wonder why I wasn't sharing my genuine emotions, troubles, successes, and thoughts more openly. He might even feel as if I didn't care enough to be honest or to take the time to really sit down with him to share what was going on in my life.

If those emotions are possible for my dad, why not consider our manner when we pray and speak to our Heavenly Father? God desires to have a close relationship with us, to hear what makes our hearts ache, to embrace us in our triumphs, and to listen to our innermost secrets. Why do we find ways to speak to him which remove that warmth and closeness? Praying is not a routine; praying is a tender time of sharing. Prayer needs no road map. It comes directly from your heart and mind to God's ear. No words are necessary. Just as your dad might have known when you were having a challenging day, so your Heavenly Father knows even more. Lean on him, praise him, and celebrate his love in your life. Moreover, share your *own* words and emotions with him.

Invite him into regular conversation every day, no matter what your specific needs may be. Remember, God has already memorized the prayers you have memorized. He is more interested in what you *really* have to say.

Focus for the Week

Let today be a fresh start for your prayers. Declutter your mind of the words that are routine, and speak from your heart. Don't worry about presentation, leaving anyone or anything out, or how long your prayer lasts. Jesus deserves every moment of your life's attention, so pray until you are done. Pray whenever you can, wherever you are, and for whatever comes to mind. Let prayer go from formal to normal. Enjoy casual sharing with your Heavenly Father and know that you always have his full attention. God is worthy of endless praise and worship, so honor him by making his relationship the one around which all others revolve.

Passages

Daniel 9:4–19
John 17:1–26
Matthew 6:5–9, 26:39

To Have Faith

To have faith in Jesus Christ is to:

> Admit imperfection.
> Have unlimited hope.
> Find comfort in his presence.
> Be in awe of him.
> Feel personally inadequate.
> Seek his forgiveness.
> Try to better yourself every day.
> Grow in the Holy Spirit.
> Be grateful for his sacrifice.
> Praise his name and Gospel.
> Humanly struggle with sin.
> Deny Satan access to your soul.
> Be thankful for his mercy.
> Give selflessly.
> Believe in his promise.
> Teach by example.
> Testify with passion.
> Understand his instructions.
> Accept his word as truth.
> Revel in eternal life.
> Speak his name to all.
> Actively pray as much as you can.
> Be joyous in serving others.
> Proclaim his generosity.
> Sing glory to him and the one who sent him.
> Submit to his will before your own.
> Know the purest of love.
> Pursue scripture and its lessons.
> Have a holy mediator before the Father.
> Honor the Savior.
> Passionately devote your life to loving him.
> Learn how to forgive.

Lift up your heart knowing that he already treasures it.
Be blessed with redemption.
Stand up for the weak.
Share your blessings and gifts with others.
Never stop stretching toward his plans for you.
Become nonjudgmental.
Include everyone in your prayers.
Know that coincidence does not exist.
Give thanks for the warrior angels protecting you.
Humbly kneel at his feet.
Acknowledge everyday miracles.
Embrace those whom others abandon.

Focus for the Week

Create your own list for Jesus in your life. It might be similar to mine, or you could use a different format such as:

"When I think of Christ, I see …"
"I show Jesus my love by …"
"I honor Christ by …"

Regardless of what form you choose, spend quiet time brainstorming about all of the descriptions of your relationship with Jesus. Your list may end up being longer than this one.

Passages

Colossians 1:4–6, 9–22
Hebrews 11

In His Eyes

When I look at myself in the mirror, I often see the negative before the positive—the weight I want to lose, the haircut that is long overdue, the fatigue in my eyes, the lack of will power to change, or the stress of the world upon my shoulders. However, when Christ looks at me, he sees everything I can't or won't. To him I am a radiant being full of love, hope, compassion, and enthusiasm. He bears witness to my potential, the true content of my heart, my joy, my dreams, and the generosity of my spirit. All that was a child in me cannot be hidden by my aging body or worried mind. It cannot be concealed because I was created in God's image. His presence in my soul will forever keep me filled with the positive qualities I require in order to glorify him and serve others during my days here.

Although I may become frustrated and endure painful experiences, my Father continues to love and embrace me as if I was still a newborn. No matter how I try, I am unable to sabotage his gifts with my own poor choices. Regardless of my shortcomings and faults, Jesus sees and accepts me as perfect, just as I am. His infinite creations come from pure righteousness, thereby guaranteeing that they are as he willed them to be. Who am I to criticize his work because of my own insecurities or lack of self-discipline? Perhaps, I should try to see myself more as he does, instead of focusing on "fixing" aspects of my person that feel substandard according to my personal set of expectations.

Please give me your eyes, Lord, that I may see more of my inner you. Also, help me to connect with you in others, that I may avoid getting caught up in their harsh self-judgment and condemnation. Thank you, Lord, for valuing our lives so much that you put us before yourself. You are forever faithful and true and have given each of us the tools we need to do your will and to return home to your eternal kingdom. Let me not waste any more time neglecting the tools or myself in our journey together.

Focus for the Week

Compose a list of everything about yourself that displeases you, leaves you feeling inadequate, or makes you critical or things you just don't like. Be as specific as you can. Make the list as long as you can. Once completed, whether in an hour or over a couple of days, find a fireplace or sink and burn the paper. Know that God already understands how you feel about yourself, but he loves you based on his own terms, not by how you see yourself. (Thank goodness!) Remember that your own criticisms will never change the part of God's being upon which you were created. Repeat this process as often as you like. Visualize God's cleansing, healing warmth accepting you "as is" each time. He loves you no matter how miserable or down in the dumps you feel. He's waiting for you to snap out of it and find the joy in life again, so get moving!

Passages

2 Corinthians 4:4–10
Genesis 1:26–27

As Simple as Cause and Effect

As the conflicts around the world escalate in number and severity, the frequency of my prayers for mankind increases. They are not exclusively for Christians or Americans, but I include all people, since the entire world desperately needs the salvation that Jesus offers.

I am very interested in world faiths, in particular the relationship between some of the followers of Judaism and some who claim Christianity as their faith. Specifically, I am curious about the degree of animosity that exists between these two populations.

In the Bible's Pentateuch, the first five books of the Old Testament, we are given a description of everything from creation to the lineage of Abraham, to prophecies of a Savior to come. God demonstrates his love for the people with whom he has chosen to share a sacred covenant, but he also shows man his wrath and justice when his people stray from his commandments in thought, word, and deed. Every step of the way, Jews recorded instructions from God, the history of the Tabernacle, the reign of kings, wars between nations, and the growth of man's relationship with his almighty Father. What a precious gift! God even provides details through prophecies of the one who is to come and offer everlasting life to everyone. He makes an offer and promise that extends to each man, woman, and child, without exception.

So, for many generations the Jewish population waited for this person to appear. When he finally arrived, many of the Jews who held religious positions of authority challenged, criticized, taunted, threatened, and rebuked his teachings and example. The miracles he performed were consistently denied the appropriate attention, respect, and awe they were due. Jesus who was born and died a Jew, who followed more of the Jewish-written laws (mitzvahs) than any other human being before or after his time, and who perfectly fulfilled all of the Old Testament prophecies continued to be rejected by those in positions of power. His actions seemed to threaten the balance of power and the laws that the leaders had established.

Yet there were multitudes of Jews and Gentiles (non-Jewish individuals) who listened to Christ's lessons, witnessed his miracles, and were amazed and believed. Some Jews and Gentiles professed their faith, though they had not actually seen Jesus in person but had only heard of his works. When Christ moved into his final days of life on Earth, the throngs of people who gathered against him, most of whom were Jewish, chose for him to be put to death over other, more severely-sentenced criminals. As Christians, we know the rest of the details surrounding his death and resurrection. My interest lies in the offence that Jews seem to take with this historical account and, on the opposite end, the blame that some Christians feel is necessary toward the Jews. I believe that both groups are missing the point.

God's will demanded a perfect, human sacrifice to atone for mankind's sins, from Adam to the end of the world. This offer and its implications of hope for a planet covered in sin are testament of God's love and desire to forgive us and save our souls from an eternity of pain, suffering, and torment. Though voluntary, Jesus' death was required, and he knew this and gave his life up willingly. Therefore, it is a simple matter of cause and effect. The Jews, as a people, could not accept Christ as their Savior. If they had recognized him as the Messiah, they never would have allowed him to be crucified. Had his crucifixion never occurred, mankind would have been denied salvation, and God's perfect will would not have been fulfilled. So, the Jews played an essential role in the glorification of Jesus. They ensured that everyone who had lived before, during, and after his time would have an invitation to reap the rewards of his selfless sacrifice. The Jews had an active part in guaranteeing their own opportunity for salvation.

Don't Christians understand that we should be grateful instead of blaming the Jews for Christ's suffering? Do you honestly believe that any part of God's will was a mistake? There are no coincidences, as the name Israel proves. God selected this name for his people, and it translates into "one who struggles with

God." His plan is flawless, so why do we feel it is our place to judge and condemn? The Jews were chosen by God to do other important things in history, and logic seems to dictate that he would include them in his Son's life, including as witnesses to the fulfillment of all of the prophecies regarding his coming, his birth, and his death. Jesus' death had to be for everyone without condition. He didn't offer his life and suffering just for those people over there, or for the poor, or for individuals with "good" records. It was an all-or-none situation.

The Jews are still waiting for the return of their Messiah, and that is their choice and set of beliefs. My hope is that they will eventually have their blindness lifted, their ears opened, their hearts softened, and their minds attuned to the words and presence of God's Son.

Jesus told a group of Jewish leaders that they could not know his Father because they did not know him. I believe he said this because the Jews of that day and age were consumed with following their own laws, and Christ did not fit into their mold. However, today is a new day, and Jesus' invitation remains with love and devotion to his family. He will be coming, again, but for some, it may require his awesome, physical presence for them to truly see and understand. Until then I will continue to appreciate the role that the Jews have in my faith, and I will honor God's will and reasoning for the ongoing separation between Jews and Christians. As always, I will keep praying for everyone.

Focus for the Week

Historically, many groups have had roles that varied in responsibility, duration, and legacy. However, there are no coincidences or people on this planet for whom God lacks purpose. Therefore, each of us is essential. Though the reason or plan may be hidden from us, every life decision, prayer, and gift made in his name will glorify him while defining our purpose. Regardless of what effects your faith has on your fellow man, Christ will be the only one whose opinion or perception matters. So, concentrate on making God your priority, and your relationships with others will be the best that you and God can make them.

Passages

Acts 3:18–26
Genesis 17:1–9
Mark 15:1–15

Quiet the Distractions

In this day and age of palm pilots, fast food, and the Internet, our attention spans bounce from place to place and task to task every other minute. We fill our days (or overbook, depending on your level of motivation) with activities well in advance, and God ends up being the appointment to be "worked in," if acknowledged at all. People's (Christians', too) internal calendars and agendas have pushed Christ aside and made him secondary to the chaos around us. However, Jesus should be the foundation upon which the rest of our day is based, whether project, telephone call, errand, or chore. We need to commit our waking hours to his name. Even the smallest act has the potential to be pleasing in God's eyes, as we continue to seek his guidance and remain grateful for our blessings. How do we see him amidst the distractions and craziness in our lives?

Instead of approaching a day as a list of "To Dos," perhaps we should view the list as a road map for ways to glorify God's presence in our lives. Even if you feel that your career leaves something to be desired, it is still filled with opportunities to praise our Lord and serve others at the same time. As a secretary, I have stopped during my stressful daily routine and asked Jesus to help me do the best work I can through him and as an assistant to my coworkers. Also, I take time to thank him for the friendship that I share with most of my fellow employees, since they have watched over me in many ways. Furthermore, I am grateful for the financial support and medical benefits that he provides through my employment.

I believe that God is much more interested in where our hearts are, with respect to our efforts and careers, than what we actually accomplish or achieve in those positions. He would probably prefer a few, faithful followers who hold positions considered low by society than have a stadium full of top executives and moneymakers whose hearts are lacking faith. Regardless of how your labors may or may not be rewarded during your time here, you may rest assured that Jesus will remember and reward every gesture that you dedicated to someone in his name, no matter how unnoticed or insignificant. From this perspective, God's gift of each day can easily be transformed into many small presents we can give right back to him. Take time to quiet the distractions and focus on what is important or, in this case, *who* is important. Devote every aspect of your day to praising his holy name, whether you are at a gas station, ball game, the office, or a Laundromat. Every place, time, and deed can honor him. Make the rest of your schedule respect his presence. He should be the only priority on your calendar.

Focus for the Week

Emphasize quality over quantity of prayer and service this week. Remember that God's time with you is precious and should not be treated as an afterthought. See how often you can praise his name through your feelings, words, and actions during daily work and miscellaneous tasks. Distractions' effectiveness depends on the time and energy you give them. Shut out people and events that take your attention away from him or create negative thoughts. Live in the victory of God's love with purpose and focus.

Passages

Ephesians 4
1 Timothy 6:1–19

Panic: The Path away from Christ

Panic has controlled my life this month. It is camouflaged in many ways. First, I recently discovered that an injury I sustained at work resulted in a herniated disc in my back, thereby changing my ability to do daily chores and participate in almost every physical activity involving sports or hard labor and varying my level of general comfort and ability to sit. Also, one of our dogs has been sick from an unknown cause for the last week, and his playmate has been struggling through seven fused vertebrae and two dysplastic hips that could go any day. In addition, my husband and I are starting to seriously consider putting our house on the market for various reasons, including all of the flights of stairs that are difficult for me to navigate with my injury, the inability of one of our dogs to climb them, cleaning and paying a mortgage for many rooms that we don't use, and the fact that our mortgage rate will increase by two percent several months from now. Furthermore, we are financially challenged due to my husband's partnership in a new business. Although its growth is promising, the venture is still young, and the income cannot compare to that of corporate America.

Lately, I wake from wild and crazy dreams of chaos and stressful situations to find the anxiety and fear welling up in my stomach and throat. These panic attacks often keep me from sleeping restfully through the night. Someone once told me that you hold your fear in your stomach. From my own experience, I believe that statement is completely accurate. I have also been spending my days suppressing the urge to cry and trying to calm my heart's rapid pace.

After several days of restlessness and prayer, I remembered an e-mail that a friend had sent me not long ago. The attachment was a checklist for faith, and the very first item listed read "the key to faith is to not panic." I laughed when I initially read it, since my life was at a much smoother part of the road. However, that statement holds new significance for me today.

When does panic rear its ugly head in my life? The answer is simple to identify and hard to process—during a time when I am aware of my lack of control. Personally, I had recently lost control of my physical health, daily routine, and ability to do recreational activities. I have no control of my dogs' longevity and well-being, short of feeding, walking, and vetting them. I certainly cannot control our household income, especially since my spare time is spent keeping the house running, making a second job out of the question. Getting the house ready to sell requires an able-bodied person to paint, get up on ladders and chairs, shovel and do weeding, mow and trim, and lift the clutter and those packed boxes into their proper places. At least I can still do laundry and dishes, though very slowly and carefully. Everywhere I turn, I feel like I am looking at an insurmountable number of obstacles and impossibilities.

The flip side of panic is trust by faith. God knows what you need, when you need, and why you need. To trust is to acknowledge your silliness in thinking you were ever *actually* in control of the situations that caused you angst. In order to quell the urge to panic, you must give Jesus your burden of fear, doubt, concern, and insecurity. Believe in his guidance. This does not guarantee that the path will be an uneventful or comfortable one, but you can rest assured that you will not be mislead or further deceived by the chaos. On the other hand, you can go very wrong by assuming that you really *are* in control of your life. Not only is this arrogant in the presence of God, but also you can't have it both ways. Either you give up your will to his, or you forever flounder in your futile attempts to override God's mission for you.

Surrendering the wheel on the road of your life is tough, but peace is found in Christ's direction for your soul. He doesn't want you to be miserable and feel like you are taking a beating from the world. His desire is to help soften the bumpy and rough times so you can get to another smooth stretch of highway. When I find myself mentally crunching the numbers in our budget for the hundredth time, or wondering how long our older dog will be with us, or fearing that my injury will not heal the way I want it to, or worrying about whether we will ever find a more affordable home, or not knowing if we will be able to sell our current house, I have to stop feeding the fear. God did not create us to fear, so I constantly struggle to hand my concerns back up to him. Since I can't have it both ways, I'd rather have it his way. I am confident that he will take care of everything. My stomach agrees.

Focus for the Week

What makes you panic? Does the panic come in short bursts, does it build over a long period of time, or does it jerk you out of a deep sleep? Does your stomach hurt, even to the touch? If you identify with my questions, then you know the misery of panic. No one can rationalize your problems away, but Jesus has offered to help you deal with them. So *let him*. Relinquish the death grip you have on your life and allow him to soothe your fear and insecurity. When you are able to do this, the pain in your stomach (neck, head, etc.) will fade. Trust his love by handing over the reins to your life. He is eager to lighten your burden.

Passages

Jeremiah 17:7–14
Matthew 6:25–34
Psalms 18:1–3
2 Timothy 1:7

A Rock-Throwing Society

Everyone does it. Some people actually say these things aloud. Others let them fester and brew within their own minds. I am guilty of doing it.

What is this mystery club to which we belong? It's the Organization for the Hopelessly Judgmental. Our nature encourages us to constantly hurl invisible stones at one another, whether spoken or silent, casting judgment upon those around us. We spend incredible amounts of time sizing people up—their hair, clothes, posture, vocabulary, attitude, income, spouse, transportation, job, eating habits, religion, manners, attractiveness, and friends. The poetic justice for all of our condemning, critiquing, and judging of others is that, in doing so, we are heaping Christ's righteous judgment upon our own heads.

Jesus holds us equally accountable for what comes out of hearts and minds as the things we say and do. The "I never said that" excuse holds no water in his court. Perhaps, if we spent more time being grateful for who we are and what we have, we would not be so focused on knocking others down based on our perceptions.

When I hear someone say that an individual who lives on the street should get a job, as if there were no logical reason for a person to have no home, job, food, or clothing, I cringe. Yes, some people have choices and make poor ones or prefer to stay where they are. Others are motivated but lack the resources. However, I know personally of a situation where a successful and well-educated, businessperson with a family and apparent happiness ended up on the street due to a nasty divorce. The spouse took literally everything, and this person was left without access to the family home and to the children. To look at this person, you might immediately decide, like much of the country, to tuck this person in the box marked "lazy" or "bum" in your mind. You wouldn't think twice of slapping the cliché label, meant for a faceless form seen in movies or on television, as side notes to life.

But, this person's pain and journey are far from the casual observer's awareness or comprehension.

Beware the labeling of others and the assumption that you know them or know of the paths that brought them to this moment in time—for you have not been given the right to pass judgment. If I feel the urge or notice my condescending tendencies (habits I am desperately trying to dismantle) rising up, I try to picture the person(s) to whom I'm speaking in a situation that would evoke compassion or pity for them instead of negative and critical thoughts. I struggle with this aspect of my life every day; however, no one is blameless in this department of human interaction. Where I am trying to change my ways, many people revel in the feeling of superiority they experience by mentally or emotionally knocking others down a few rungs on the ladder. I think that they do so because it keeps them busy enough not to have to methodically examine their own lives and habits before God.

God pays very careful attention to all of your judgments, even those that are never seen or heard. He keeps extremely accurate records, and the day is approaching when Jesus' will decide the consequences for your life's sin and fruit. Spend the days you have left as judgment free as you can, since those thoughts and actions will only further burden you when you go before him. This is not to say that you have to agree with or condone the decisions, actions, words, and/or views of those around you. However, you must leave the consequences for these situations to him.

Focus for the Week

Select one person who sits at the top of your list of judgments. Instead of sizing them up this week and consequently letting them irritate you, focus your efforts on letting go and trusting God to take care of it. By doing so, you accomplish two things: (1) you are decreasing the number of criticisms heaped upon your head and (2) you are freeing up time and attention that is better spent with Jesus, improving you as a spiritual being and acknowledging that it's not your place to condemn another's words or actions. We have become arrogant in our desire to insert our own authority before God's righteousness. Use your prayers and time to focus on your own shortcomings and ask Christ to strengthen you, allowing the criticisms that you have of other people to dwindle in your mind and heart.

Passages

Ezekiel 7:3–8
Romans 14:10–13

Servanthood: An Inspiration and Dedication to Love

Christ spent his life serving those whom he loved. Servanthood is a state of mind that is made up of complete humility, selflessness, and compassion. Being a servant of God requires two things: devoting your life to Jesus and a willingness to put others before yourself in the context of that service.

Servanthood seems to be the antithesis of society's nature of "me, first," "what's in it for me," and "only if it's in my best interest." Christ's life and death made it all about him. His perfect days and nights demonstrated how God intended for man to treat man. He embraced his family with a perspective that never wavered from loyal, steadfast giving.

We need to adopt this stature, both in spirit and action, in order to grow closer to Jesus. Going through the motions without possessing the sincerity and heartfelt yearning to connect with our Savior leaves us empty, even though a kind deed was done. Jesus told us that first and foremost we are to love our God with all our hearts. Loving our neighbors and the consequent actions, gifts, and prayers we extend to our neighbors represent the fruit that we bear *because* of our love for Jesus. The second without the first is unsustaining.

Servanthood demands that we willingly assume the lowest rung on life's ladder with graciousness, since we know that Christ will determine where our final place shall be. No score is kept; only man's love of God and love of his fellow man need be noted by Jesus.

Serving can take many forms. Following are a few ideas that might help you put service into action. Use them to celebrate Christ's name and his precious spirit. Ask him to help you find a deeper appreciation for the ability and calling to serve.

Ideas

- Provide a meal for someone in need.
- Make time to listen.
- Let someone out in busy traffic.
- Pray for a person who seems upset, lost, or lonely.
- Donate something that has personal meaning to you.
- Stop to help with a stalled car, a spilled grocery bag, an injured person, or an abandoned animal.
- Give someone a lift.
- Give a genuine compliment.
- Recognize others' efforts, regardless of type or duration.
- Take someone who needs shelter into your home.
- Keep your eyes and ears open to help others find work.
- Babysit for free.
- Work or volunteer for a charitable organization.
- Invite a street person to share a meal with you.
- Clean the home of someone who is sick, hospitalized, or grieving the loss of a loved one.
- After a storm, help a community clean its yards and streets.
- Do yard work for those who cannot do for themselves.
- Spend time thinking positive thoughts and praying for those around you.
- Be an example of God's hope and love, even during a hard day.
- Play with children but also be a model of servanthood and kindness for them.
- Pray for humility, that you may constantly be Christ's servant, even in the absence of men to serve.

Focus for the Week

Create your own list of ideas, or add to mine. Try to incorporate at least one idea into each day of this week. Let your list be open-ended so you can continue to add thoughts as they come to mind or as the need arises. Remember that the list is an extension of your love for Jesus. These good deeds can never be a substitute for the time he wants to spend with you personally, through your prayers and love. Make time with him before you share time with others.

Passages

Joshua 22:5
Luke 7:44–48

No Substitutions, Please

The world has witnessed amazingly devoted Christians over thousands of years. We have labeled said individuals as Disciples (then Apostles), saints, martyrs, and relatives of Christ (Mary, Joseph, Elizabeth, and so on). Growing up, I learned about these people and their roles in history, but I experienced significant discomfort in being taught that prayers should be directed to them, in addition to those that we send our Father, Jesus, and the Holy Spirit. As an adult, my maturing faith led me back to scripture for an explanation and evidence as to why I should be praying to these elite Christians. Within scripture I found just the opposite. Though the Bible describes various aspects of the lives of the aforementioned people, I did not find instructions from God, Jesus, or the Holy Spirit that we need to send them our prayers. All of these people demonstrated their devotion to God through their actions and words, but I was unable to find justification that warranted prayer. As a matter of fact, even the angels who were messengers to mankind shirked when humans fell before them to worship. They diligently reminded God's followers that only the Trinity deserved worship and praise.

If angels understand, why don't we? Hence, this is my confusion. Today, we have designated specific deceased Christians to aide us during difficult times, protect us from harm, find a missing possession, keep us from getting lost, or heal us from an illness. Regardless of their esteem while here on Earth, in heaven these same people will be standing before God and his Son, side-by-side with even the meekest of believers. Celebrating how someone honored our Savior through his or her life is one thing, but praying to him or her for guidance is a whole different ball game. God has told us over and over not to put idols before him. Idols are not only tangible objects, but they can also be people and ideas as well.

I'm not saying that these followers lack importance of stature or that they lead unimpressive lives. Obviously, they exhibited loyalty, faith, and commitment of tremendous magnitude. However, they were still just people. Mother Theresa is the person, during my lifetime, who exhibited the most amazing selflessness, generosity, strength of character, and passion for faith of anyone I've ever seen—but I don't pray to her. I have lost several family members dear to my heart, most of whom modeled their steadfast faith and trust in God. Sometimes, I talk to them and long to see them again, but I don't pray to them. Beware of anyone who elevates his stature to either between you and Christ or beside Christ. Jesus did not designate any liaisons between man and the Trinity. We are all spectators and participants in our relationship with the Almighty, and there are no substitutes for the receiver of our prayers.

Our souls are connected to the Father, Son, and Holy Spirit. Only the Trinity can nurture, encourage, comfort, and enrich our spiritual selves. Only the one, true source of love and righteousness can sustain us. We need to remind ourselves that those who have been lifted up and worshipped, being examples of dedicated Christians, simply demonstrate that anyone has the potential to grow closer to God during their time here. With that in mind, our single model of an ideal life remains Jesus' time with us. His life was perfect in every way, and his life will be the one by which we are judged. He told us that no one reaches the Father, except through him. His family, friends, and followers must take the same path that we do. No exceptions, refunds, substitutions, or excuses accepted.

Focus for the Week

How often do you find yourself revering someone or something other than God? Even though we aren't intentionally avoiding approaching the Lord directly, our actions go against his commandments. We cannot seek guidance or blessings from other historical figures without worshipping idols in the process, since we attribute ultimate power and judgment to those individuals when God alone is supreme. Spend this week removing the idols and methods of thinking that rely on anyone other than Christ for support or intervention. Recognize that everything flows through him, and seek out his forgiveness for the times that you sought assistance elsewhere. Turn back to his perfect wisdom and will.

Passages

Acts 17:16–30
1 John 5:17–21

The "Closeness-to-God" Game

We, Christians, are all players in the game that I like to call the "Closeness-to-God" game. Usually, each person considers himself to be the main challenger searching to define his relationship with God based solely on his observations of others. We are doomed to forever lose this game, since our lives constantly bear witness to those who give more money in the collection plate, have read much more of the Bible, donate more personal goods to the poor, volunteer for more charitable organizations, pray more often, and complain less often than we do. If a winning formula isn't possible, then why is it so difficult to shut off these habits of comparison?

Perhaps, our tendencies lie in society's continued perpetuation of basing our measure of faith and closeness to God by using a checklist of actions instead of our hearts' promises and commitments to him. Humans have always judged each other and compared themselves across many categories. However, God's relationship with us is measured by an exclusive set of standards—most of which are not manifested through observable behaviors. His love for us does not grow or diminish in time, though he knows our true selves, flaws and all. So, trying to place oneself somewhere on a scale of faith with everyone else who believes in God would be like trying to decide which grain of sand on the Earth is closest to the Milky Way. Though God's spirit has enveloped us since before our parents even knew us, we are infinitely distant from him by our own choosing. The only intimacy we may ever achieve, to our Heavenly Father, comes from a single source, his Son.

Jesus' love and sacrifice offer us an eternity of celebration with him and his Father. Where the distance between man and God is never-ending, Jesus bridges that abyss in the blink of an eye. Where we grains of sand fall in comparison to one another is irrelevant. The winning solution for the "Closeness-to-God" game cannot be found by looking around oneself. The answer lies in searching inward and upward.

Focus for the Week

Think about the people to whom you compare your faith. Is there a particular acquaintance, friend, or family member who seems to be so much closer to God than you are? Do you find yourself longing to follow his or her lead, by doing more of what he or she does in prayer, reading, and daily worship? Now just hold it right there! The only visions you need remember are the practices of Jesus. Of course, we weren't actually present during his life, but his example and teachings are what you need to follow. No person in your daily life is worthy of being a model in his place, nor can they be a substitute for his passion and dedication to your soul. The phrase "what would Jesus do" has become almost cliché in today's world, yet it gets to the truth of the matter. Regardless of how much your fellow man wows you with his faith-filled practices, he is still only a member (not the coach) of Christ's team. Instead, examine Christ's life to search for instruction on how you can enrich your relationship with the Almighty. This week, pick five faith-related points on which you want to focus and write them down. Use Christ's example when you decide to put them into action.

Passages

2 Corinthians 10:12–18
Matthew 12:42–50

Friendship Revealed

As life progresses through different stages, your peer group changes, as does your appearance, priorities, and passions. Nothing is promised today and guaranteed again tomorrow. That is why friends are such spectacular miracles in one's life. God has provided us with relationships that step outside altogether of family baggage, societal rankings, and the rulebook. These personal, fan club members honestly believe in you, your potential, blunders, and inadequacies, and they do so in love. The bonds that link true friends cannot be severed by a simple disagreement or offence. No distance can extinguish the fierce loyalty and devotion that inspires friends to encourage and counsel one another, hopefully to heal injuries, bear challenges, and celebrate successes.

A genuine friend does not gauge the substance of your relationship based on the number of telephone calls, e-mails, or get-togethers. The foundation of friendship is built upon steadfast trust and concern, reciprocated equally by both individuals, regardless of time, place, or reason. These incredible people hold fast and protectively to your moments of vulnerability and intimate sharing. No word or oath need be spoken to ensure your confidence and lack of judgment through life's trials and tribulations, yet no other sound or voice can be heard over a friend's shout for joy for your triumphs and conquering achievements.

Imagine your dearest confidant for a minute. See the person's face. Hear his or her voice. Remember his or her gentle hug. Experience the inner peace, excitement, comfort, and happiness that seeing your friend brings to mind. Christ desires this exact type of relationship with you—one of depth and commitment. He wants to share in all aspects of your life, but it need not always be through the formality of prayer. Sing out to him when something fabulous comes across your path. Cry to him when you are hurting and need someone to listen. Speak to him of nervousness before a job interview or birth of a child. Ask him for advice when you are confused and require assistance. Reach out to him, since he yearns to be your best friend, not just as a social acquaintance, but as a spiritual companion.

Friends will come and go for various reasons, but usually their presence teaches you to grow in ways that you might not have otherwise. Jesus will never pass through your life, and you may rest assured that he remains constant in his love for you. So, treasure and nurture those valuable and unique friendships, since he handpicked each one according to what support and encouragement you would need most.

Focus for the Week

Make a list of five events going on in your life. They might be exciting, scary, intimidating, fantastic, or nerve-wracking. Share each of these with Christ, either aloud or in the silence of your heart. Tell him what you're going through, just as you would with your best friend. Know that he wants to offer his friendship through all of your personal experiences, easy or tough. Try to remember to include him in daily activities as well because his companionship lasts forever. Your life may not be glamorous or notable by your own standards, but his desire to support you overrides your personal opinions. Involve him in your triumphs and failures, celebrations and mourning, and the possibilities and struggles. Lean on him.

Passages

John 15:12–16
Luke 11:5–10

Baptism Confusion

As far back as my childhood, I remember images of baptism—priests pouring water on babies' foreheads and adults being dunked in lakes and water tanks pop into my mind. I learned very early that baptism cleansed a person of his or her sin. I freely accepted this explanation, as most Christians do after years of repeatedly hearing the same message. As I grew older, the clarity of this process seemed to blur, and by the time I graduated from college, I found the stereotypical opinion of what baptism represented to feel incomplete. The Christians seemed to agree that Jesus had been baptized and forgiveness took place, though only a few claimed to know from what or why.

I decided to examine scripture to find a more thorough explanation, and I also spent time talking to friends, fellow churchgoers, and people in my Bible study group. After much prayer and ruminating, I began to ask some basic questions and used them to research and find the best answers that I could from scripture and my fellow Christians.

1. What is physical baptism? Baptism is the symbolic acceptance of responsibility for one's sins and repentance for those sins through Christ, thereby being cleansed by God's grace via the Holy Spirit's entering your heart, mind, and soul.
2. If you must be a sinner to be baptized, why did Jesus have John baptize him? Jesus did not need to be baptized. He was sinless and blameless before his Father and man. Perhaps, he realized that men wouldn't be able to grasp the concept of the Holy Spirit's entering their bodies and "washing" away their sins through repentance. His baptism was a demonstration for man to help them comprehend the idea at some level. The Bible contains conversations regarding whether baptism is of God or of man. Although man goes through the physical motions, the

invitation of the Holy Spirit into one's being is of God. At Christ's baptism when God sent the dove down to Jesus, claimed Jesus was his Son, and said he was pleased with him, I believe he said this so that man could bear witness to what Jesus was doing and clearly see that the power of forgiveness went far beyond the actions of man and the water that he used.

3. Why are babies baptized? This practice still baffles me. If baptism requires repentance and the asking of Christ's mercy, shouldn't we be old enough to be aware of our sin, its absolute wrongness, Christ's sacrifice for our eternal lives, and the necessity for forgiveness? I have often heard that humans are "born into sin" by nature, in that none of us is perfect and all of us are sinners. I agree with the lack of perfection in the human race. However, I find significance in the fact that in biblical history the symbolic shift from youth to adulthood took place as Jewish youth reached their teens. Christ was a mature adult when he was baptized. Maybe age was more of a factor since the children were permitted time to come to know, accept, honor, and respect God and his power. Even after Christ's birth, Jesus called the children to him freely, without condition or hesitation. If anything, I believe that infants are probably the most innocent humans in God's care because their capacity to develop sinful thoughts and behaviors is limited by their helplessness and lack of higher-order thinking. Sinning is a learned behavior, and though sinning is not difficult, acknowledging the need for repentance and asking Jesus for his forgiveness take much effort and accountability. Only as children age and spend time building a relationship with Christ will they come to understand the importance of telling God they are sorry. Perhaps, parents wish to baptize their children to ask God's blessing and protection upon their lives instead of intending it to be for forgiveness of sins.

4. Is baptism necessary? Baptism by the Holy Spirit is essential in any Christian's life. However, the symbolic baptism of someone in a church or holy place is simply that—symbolic. For some people, especially children, the actual procedure may be more distracting than it is contemplative. (I have seen similarities in marriage celebrations that get swept aside in the wake of wedding festivities.) Others hope to mark the occasion so that family and friends can honor a person's growth and ongoing commitment to Christ. I guess the two aspects of baptism I want my future children to firmly understand are these: Christ's love and forgiveness can come into your heart anytime and anywhere through the Holy Spirit when you genuinely ask it to enter, and the most important point to remember when asking for forgiveness is that you are truly sorry for what you have done and you promise to try avoid repeating the sins you have committed.

5. Does where you are baptized, or by whom, matter? I believe the answer is "no." When it comes down to it, the Holy Spirit does not schedule its arrival based on special church services or celebrations noted on your home calendar. Baptism is not exclusively affiliated with any particular denomination or location. The only two participants are you and Jesus (through the Holy Spirit)—no exceptions! Consequently, there may be many symbolic baptisms going on across the world where the Holy Spirit is absent, just as the Holy Spirit may be very busy working in the hearts of those who have never formally belonged to or been baptized in a church. So be it. Every individual should focus on his own need for repentance and let God handle everyone else's paths to forgiveness. After all, he is the expert.

Focus for the Week

Think about your own experiences with baptism. Do you feel like you have genuinely asked God's spirit to reside in your heart, mind, and soul? If so, was a baptism with water required in order for it to happen, or did it occur without any type of formal demonstration? If not, what do you think you can do to extend yourself to Christ and invite him into your life? Are you prepared to constantly humble yourself before him, ask for his forgiveness, and struggle every day to live a life pleasing to him? In addition, consider how you can distinguish between symbolic practices and your intimate and sincere relationship with God.

Passages

Matthew 3:4–17
Romans 6:3–11

Overcoming Pain and Disappointment

How many times do we feel let down when anticipated events don't go our way? The significance of the event may vary, but the sense of pain and disappointment can seem tremendous. I had a particularly emotional letdown today. For the first time in two years of hoping, I thought I was finally pregnant. Amidst my husband's and my schedules, overwhelming stresses, and full-time jobs, we had seen very little of one another, but we kept asking the Lord to bless us with children. Our dream is to have a family that will grow to love God, to know his name, and to praise and worship him each day.

Anyway, today brought the images and dreams of tiny socks, lullabies, pacifiers, and the baby "smell" to another abrupt close. My heart ached, and my tears flowed. As devastated as I felt, and though I cried for several hours, my faith assures me that Jesus is watching over us and waiting for the best time for our family to bloom. Perhaps, the delay is required to prepare for a healthy baby, financial security, or relocation to a different home. Regardless of the reason for his timing, I try to cope with the repeated disappointments by looking for positive aspects in these situations. I cannot possibly see God's logic in any given scenario, but I continue to reach out to him for comfort and reassurance. As much as I ache and grieve for the child that will not be today, I know that Christ is beside me with loving counsel. Seeking out the positive in the negative goes against human nature, but trying to do so can improve our relationship with Jesus. By recognizing and acknowledging his wisdom and plan for our lives, we submit ourselves to following his will. We believe without seeing or knowing what is in store. We trust that, though we feel like we are flying through the air out of control, his strong hands deftly catch our flailing bodies with confidence and ease. However, we are not immune to the pain and suffering that accompanies traumatic events in our lives. The important part is how we get through them.

This day is only one of many in my life, but I will remember the hurt I experienced for a long time. Regardless of your own disappointments and pain, whether from a job loss, relationship change, death of a loved one, injury, abandonment, handicap, loneliness, abuse, spiritual isolation, miscarriage, or depression, believe in the one who cherishes you and wishes to carry you through the difficult times. Without him, we would wander in darkness and misery. He is our hope—always.

Focus for the Week

Pick a time in your life (past or present) when you were in pain or experiencing a significant disappointment. How did you cope? Did it affect your relationship with Christ? How? How long did it take you to heal, or are you still trying to recover? Even though these events sometimes make us feel helpless, like a target, unfairly treated, or seeking justice, God already knows what we are thinking or that we are mourning. We exist in a mere speck of God's time within creation. To us in the moment, it seems monumental and insurmountable, but he already knows that we will eventually heal. Tell him of your pain. He is ready to listen and give you the grace and peace you desire.

Passages

John 15:26–16:11
Romans 8:10–18
Philippians 4:13

The Master Gourmet

Tonight, I've got food on the brain, so I am exploring God's wonder in what I eat. Upon many occasions, I've strolled through parts of my local grocery store and marveled at the menu that God provides for my health and pleasure. The aroma of fresh strawberries lures me to the berry counter, only to tease me with the sight of plump and juicy blueberries and blackberries. Soft avocados, firm tomatoes on the vine, fresh silver queen corn still in its husk, and sweet melons galore bring so much of God's love to my table. Lacking self-discipline, I usually cover the entire conveyor belt in the checkout line with a little bit of everything from the produce department, whether fruit, vegetable, or nut. In my moments of food reflection, I realize that we hurry through our food in many ways. I am going to make a conscious effort to slow down and enjoy my meals and snacks with more attention and appreciation.

Have you ever really looked at your food? I mean other than when you buy it and before you quickly put it into your mouth. Do you inhale its fragrance? Natural foods amaze me. Pink grapefruit ranks as one of my top five favorites. I love the faint smell of citrus that comes from the skin. My fingers enjoy the smooth, but subtly grainy, texture of the peel. The inside holds hundreds (maybe thousands) of pieces of tart, juicy pulp that all fit together in an ideal package. The shades of pink vary from the center to the rind, displaying shiny pales to hot fuchsia. I can't decide if I like the pulp or juice better. I'll just call it a tie, for now.

The strange thing about eating is that most people treat meals as obligations instead of adventures. God's gift of food presents us with an incredible array of unique tastes, scents, textures, and responses to his menu. No two fruits, veggies, nuts, or meats are exactly the same. Therefore, every dining experience opens the door to a new way of examining "the same old thing" on your plate.

Perhaps, when we ask God to bless our food, we should take more time to recognize and explore exactly how much miraculous thought, creativity, and love went into our seemingly average, everyday meals. These ensembles of expertly crafted, nutritious elements exist for the sole purpose of providing sustenance for us. Not only did God give us food, but he also made our menu so extensive that no one person could possibly partake of every single food in a lifetime. In addition, natural foods contain all of the components required by the human body for proper digestion and general health. Therefore, we fit perfectly with our food. The trouble with our diets comes when we stray from the freshness of God's garden to the boxes, bags, and cans that modern-day society provides for our convenience.

The more I revel in the sensations found in my refrigerator, the more I wonder why I drifted so far away from God's handiwork. Remember, God said that our bodies are our temples. So, what are you feeding *your* temple? Is it something your body will savor, or is it something that just saves you some time?

Focus for the Week

Let this week be a feast for your senses and your faith. Use each meal as an opportunity to praise God for his gifts. Select a fresh component of your meal and really take a moment to observe and absorb its color, smell, texture, and taste. Slow down and give your meal's maker the respect and appreciation he deserves.

Passages

Exodus 16:11–27, 35
Genesis 1:11–12, 29–30

The Do, Are, and Will Be

Casual conversation etiquette dictates that you ask others about their families, careers, and pastimes. Usually, an individual leads into said conversation with "what do you do" or something similar. The funny thing is that how we answer this question can present an entirely different picture of our lives than the idea of who we *are*. The "do" segment of our lives translates into descriptions of work, errands, and miscellaneous tasks that fill our days. "Dos" are actions.

More intimate relationships permit deeper conversation into the "are" of our lives. The concept of "who are you" isn't a typical point of discussion with acquaintances, though "how are you" is commonplace enough. The "are" is more about your feelings, passions, dreams, and soul. It encompasses the dimensions of your being, how you relate to others, and most importantly your faith or lack thereof. The "are" is what is left after all of the worldly distractions and priorities are removed. Yet the "are" may not represent God's purpose for us and what we "will be." For instance, I feel like one of my gifts from God is to teach. I love being in the classroom, sharing my knowledge and passion, building up my students by showing them their own successes and potential, and believing that life lessons are just as important, if not more important, than the textbook ones. I was blessed to be a classroom teacher for almost ten years. I was privileged because my "do" and "are" overlapped. However, I had to leave teaching when my employer required more and more certifications, expectations, and responsibilities on top of my seventy-hour workweeks.

My passion was still healthy, but the career continued to become increasingly unhealthy. My husband and I discussed the growing stress and demands of the position, and we decided that I needed to retire for the sake of my own physical, emotional, and spiritual well-being. Over the last decade, we had hardly spent an evening or weekend together when I wasn't grading papers, planning, creating worksheets or tests, or calculating final averages. I felt positive about the decision, but part of me seemed lost without the spark that ignited behind those closed classroom doors. The freedom to give, laugh, and challenge had coaxed me out of bed early each morning for many years, and now I had to try and find my way into an entirely new "do." I promised my students that I would remain available for tutoring should they still need me, but I began searching for a healthier job—one with a normal schedule, time to actually eat lunch without running around and taking charge, and without lugging a bottomless bag of work home each night. I began to wonder what God intended for my "will be" to be. I had always held true to teaching being the single thing that God sent me here to do. Would my lack of a classroom prevent me from my "will be"? Had I already had my "will be" and didn't know it?

I wasn't sure, but God has a way of getting you to go where he wants you to, with or without your knowledge, understanding, or planning. Anything is possible. So, I continued to work odd jobs for family and friends and search for what he had in store. During this time, I also tried to write a young adult book, since I've always had a desire to write. However, that endeavor failed to materialize. The next book I attempted was a compilation of poems, but that, too, was a bust. Having found nothing but frustration in my inability to compose anything of substance, I decided to stick to my tutoring and job search.

Over a year later, a friend and I were discussing scripture, our faith, and where we saw the world headed. At some point, I casually mentioned an opinion and idea I had for this book. She was so excited about it that she stated, several times before we hung up, that I just *had* to write it or at least start journaling and doing some brainstorming. I turned it over in my mind for a week along with the memories of my previous writing experiences, lackluster and depressing though they were. She called to ask if I'd gotten started and chastised me for not having done so. "Where do you think all of your ideas come from anyway?" she demanded of me.

After much prayer and pushing aside my feelings of inadequacy and lack of authority, I began to write. The words poured through my pen and onto the paper. I did no outlining or brainstorming. The words flowed, and they formed entire chapters at a sitting. I didn't struggle with any part of the process. I began writing on the back of bank envelopes, grocery store receipts, lined paper, plain paper, notepads, Post-its, and anything else I could find.

Best of all, I am writing about an aspect of my life that inspires the rest of it. Is this book my "will be"? Did it come out of nowhere to tackle me and show me another avenue of existence—of giving, laughing, and challenging others to examine their "dos," "ares," and "will bes"? I can't be sure, since there may be much more to come. But I am sure of one thing. Christ created something from nothing in my writing, and I am thankful and excited to see where it will lead. I joyfully anticipate the journey of this book. If these words reach even a single person with God's message, then I will be blessed in my possible "will be," for I cannot think of a greater gift than being able to share hope and passion of faith with another. Maybe, a day will come when my "do," "are," and "will be" will merge onto the same, harmonious path.

Besides, the Apostles were simple fishermen before Christ came into their lives. They probably never had an inkling, while pulling their nets out of the water and cleaning fish guts, that they would become the closest friends of the living, walking, breathing Son of God.

Focus for the Week

Make a list of five roles or goals that you would like to attain. Do these aspirations offer opportunities to reach toward God? Will they be conducive to spiritual health in addition to the responsibilities they will demand? Do you believe any of them will overlap, or do they already? As long as you keep your focus on God's will, instead of yours, and his purpose for you, instead of relying solely on your wants, your trust and his direction, wisdom, and timing will ensure that you find your "will be."

Passages

Colossians 1:9–13
Luke 9:23–27

Sales Pitch of Satan

Satan has many faces. Hollywood has renditions of creatures with horns, hoofs, and burning flesh, and even children wear his face. Recently, we received a set of DVDs that examines Satan's presence around us in daily life and today's society. My husband and I were grateful for the gift, since we had been casually aware of his works, but we hadn't spent too much time considering Satan's relationships, connections, and motives.

He has been as busy as any angel with an inferiority complex can be. We found the series to be very eye-opening as to how Satan worms his way into Christians' homes, music, fears, and relationships. Some people dismiss this type of information by claiming that spending time and energy reading, listening, and digesting it is a waste of time. However, I believe that knowing your enemy and his strategies can keep you from being an ignorant and unarmed victim. Recognizing Satan's hand in everyday life aides Christians in fighting him head-on.

According to the Bible, angels have been battling over humans' souls for thousands of years, heavenly hosts in protection of mankind and Satan's horde in its destruction. The devil tempts the weak into pledging allegiance to him through violence, blasphemy, and bloodshed. Be not deceived. The holy war that rages beyond what we can see is quite real, but the struggle is a crucial element in God's plan for his people. The final decision of choosing sides is ours to make. Herein lays the interesting sales pitch of Satan.

Consider this: God has released Satan to reign on Earth until Christ returns. Satan is furious with God for kicking him out of heaven. As he fell from grace, he took a slew of angels with him to begin building his army against the Almighty. So, what is the most effective way for him to take revenge against God? He cannot confront God, since he knows that he has no chance of winning. Therefore, he chooses an easier target, but one important to his maker: God's children, who have been given free will. Nothing is more satisfying for Satan than luring men, women, and children away from their Father. However, the ultimate victory and revenge for him lies in convincing a child of God to completely abandon this holy relationship for all eternity.

In order to do this, he creates conditional relationships with his prey. He rewards their evil deeds, showers their infidelities, selfishness, and hate with praise and profit, and shelters those who feel lost with the company of anger and ignorance. Satan has unlimited resources for his sales pitch here on Earth, but his "groupies" don't seem to "get" it. Satan doesn't love them unconditionally, as God always will. Each of their souls is simply another tally mark on Satan's scorecard. Satan's followers are nothing but pawns and soon-to-be statistics that will be joining him in the lake of fire. Yet they actually believe that their loyalty will put them in favor with the Prince of Darkness. The harsh reality is that these people are a means to an end.

His sales pitch must be incredibly effective because his followers don't seem to be the least bit panicked by their situation. They are told that "Do as Thou Wilst," the motto of Satan's "church," is the philosophy to follow. The main focus of this church is to destroy the family unit, thereby perpetuating lack of respect or concern for anyone other than oneself. Satan's followers enjoy the freedom and effortless existence that is required to live obligation-, responsibility-, and accountability-free lives. Some of these individuals have gone to the extent of creating their own faith with guidelines that promote the same type of lifestyle. On the other hand, God's followers are very concerned for Satan's groupies. Christians know that God has given Satan this time, but it will be taken from him in a fashion that will dwarf every world war in history. Unfortunately, Satan is constantly manipulating and building his army in anticipation of the illusion of future victory. Those who have been deceived don't want to think about how Satan's short-term gifts of talent, lust, power, wealth, fame, beauty, and narcissism will only last long enough for him to crunch his soul numbers. I pray for his armies that they may not be too distant in loneliness, anger, and self-indulgence to hear God's voice and step back from the fire. If not, their eternal lives will be spent in suffering and regret—all for the waste of Satan's tally mark on their heads. Lord, please have mercy on those who choose to turn to the darkness instead of to your light. Help them to be strong enough to let go of Satan's lures and empty promises and seek out your truth and fulfillment.

Focus for the Week

Pray diligently this week for those people who live behind Satan's deceptions. Actively ask Jesus to touch their hearts and minds, showing them the truth of his word. It is still not too late for men to witness the majesty and righteousness of God. Include in your prayers those who claim to have no faith or who practice other faiths. They, too, need Christ to give them eyes to see and ears to hear his message.

Passages

Chronicles 21:1–7
Job 1 and 2

Men and Fish

When Jesus spoke about the disciples becoming fishers of men, one can immediately understand the metaphor he was using. But take a moment to really compare the two groups, fish versus man. The similarities in behavior and reasoning are startlingly parallel in some ways.

For instance, fish normally congregate in groups called schools. The instinct in this is that there is safety in numbers. Mankind demonstrates the same behavior, since individuals will associate their physical presence, and often opinion, with a group in order to feel secure and accepted.

When given a tempting lure, fish will often react without thinking instead of examining the possibility of a predator lurking nearby. Men and women model this same characteristic in their words and actions when they react to others' invitations to temptation, whether the enticing factor be gossip, a personal vice, or physical lust. We do not think of humans as having a natural predator, but Satan is very real and thrives on our impulses and lack of introspection and discipline.

Another characteristic of fish is that they continue to struggle and fight against the nets and hooks that capture them, though the battle is a losing one. Even if one such catch should get lucky with a return to the sea or lake, it will sometimes die anyway, since the drive and struggle to survive was too taxing on its body. We, humans, are the same way with Christ. The more our selfish nature attempts to escape his call and desire to draw us in, the further we get from his truly freeing us. Our perception is that *we* are in control of our lives, and this philosophy prevents us from being close to Jesus. Our society tells us that if we fight against this world with enough force and determination, we can accomplish anything. Yet Christ's teachings were just the opposite. He asked us to give up all control and desire for material possessions and trust him to know what is best for us. His perfect wisdom is the only compass we need for a happy life, though it may not be filled with the worldly riches, power, and prestige we originally envisioned for ourselves.

The most important aspect of having a relationship with Jesus is that, unlike fish that are captured or released and destined to perish, believers will never have to fear death. Christ's love, suffering, and sacrifice ensured that we will share in his pain-free, guilt-free, fear-free, and carefree eternal kingdom, where we will be face-to-face with our God, serving and praising him forever. How grateful we should be to our Lord, who made it a priority to continue to seek us out through every moment of every day since he walked the earth!

God seeking after us is hardly a new concept. Jesus offered himself as the perfect sacrifice, liaison, and guide to his Father. Before Jesus' birth, God asked many men to turn their lives completely over to him. Noah probably became one of the "black sheep" of his family by constructing a large, wooden boat and stocking it with animals. Moses was told to go before Pharaoh (the man who had put a price on Moses' head) and his army and to try to bargain for the lives of the children of Israel before leading them to safety. Abraham was instructed to build an altar and sacrifice his own son to God. Had any of these men denied God, biblical history would have been significantly different. However, theirs was a time of relationship with God when believing without seeing was not necessary. God openly spoke to these men and performed miracles in their presence. However confident they may have been, their trust in God was what protected them from hunger, harm, and death.

Today, Jesus continues to pursue us based on our faith in him and his Father. For those who must see to believe, they will never be satisfied, regardless of how many miracles they witness. These individuals have to be "sold" by an idea, convinced with reasoning and evidence, and surrounded by others who support their opinion. Christians' strength is in the fact that we believe in him without seeing the wondrous demonstrations of God, Jesus, and angels or hearing the holy voices found in the Old and New Testaments. We have more than enough proof in the Bible and everyday miracles to reaffirm our confidence in and gratefulness for God's generous gifts of friendship and love. So, don't struggle and strain in your relationship with Jesus. Trust that he has something even better waiting for you.

Focus for the Week

Identify ways that you personally struggle with God. Examine why you think that these parts of your life present the perceived need for struggle. Is there a part of your life that you are having difficulty handing over into his care? Maybe it's your marriage, children, job, health, or another seriously cherished aspect of your world. Find a way to give Christ the burden of this weight. When you are ready to let go, he is willing and eager to do what you cannot. Your struggle only creates more stress for your spirit, and this stress will eventually become overwhelming. Trust that his decisions are what is best for you. Stop exhausting yourself by believing that you can be set free of challenges by your own will power.

Passages

Acts 2:1–39
Matthew 4:18–20

Faith and Optimism

I recently participated in a class that examined my emotional level of development. The course broke down human emotions into four basic categories and provided scenarios and activities in order to evaluate my responses in various situations. The subsection that addressed optimism interested me the most. Optimism means much more to me than addressing whether a glass of water is half-full or half-empty. It is not simply a perspective; it is a belief, something felt at a level beyond the analytical. Then I realized that nothing in the workbook touched upon beliefs or faith.

For me, optimism is generated from God's presence in my heart. I do not adhere to the general philosophy that things will get better only because they cannot get any worse. I know that my situation will improve because I believe in God's will and purpose for me. Though they may make me uncomfortable, difficulties in my life push me to learn and grow. Therefore, my trust and confidence in Christ perpetuate my optimism.

Improvement is relative to the one beholding it. Some people aren't happy or satisfied unless all aspects of their lives are running smoothly and according to plan. True optimism is available at any time and for every situation. An individual's world could be crumbling around them, yet he might assure loved ones or friends that all will eventually be well again. Emphasis is consciously placed on even the tiniest promising elements in one's daily life. You might say that optimism goes beyond the lemon/lemonade equation to including lemons as great skin cleaners, attractive centerpieces, and outstanding pie and trifle ingredients.

Optimism does not require any proof or incentive. It cannot blossom from a selfish place; it springs from a soul that recognizes Christ's promise, his gifts, his protection, and his desire for our contentment. With that in mind, are you someone who clings to the negative or challenging experiences in your path, expecting more trouble to follow, or are you trying to navigate the speed bumps as best you can, knowing that God is at the wheel helping you to find the open road ahead? Which person do you *want* to be?

Focus for the Week

For the next seven days, adopt an optimistic outlook when dealing with difficult times, people, or events. For you, this may mean coping without becoming depressed or angry. Optimism doesn't imply that you are smiling every moment. However, it implies that your eyes are up, seeking out God's next blessing, instead of down, looking for the next hurdle or pitfall.

Passages

Matthew 11:27–30
Romans 5:1–5

Loneliness

Everyone has experienced loneliness at some point in their lives, even though some would never admit this truth. I've had different degrees of loneliness in my short thirty-four years. I can remember back to third grade when my family moved to a new city. I had very few friends through my early primary and middle schools, and my lack of classification as an attractive, athletic, or popular student kept me socially isolated. Aspects of my loneliness were exacerbated by the emphasis placed on popularity during my high school years. I remember finding some rare solace with an eclectic group of girls on the tennis team and a handful of others with whom I could "hang out." By my sophomore year, I was so desperate to get out of the high school environment that I begged my guidance counselor to let me apply to take college courses (not an option back in those days). I didn't know how I could survive the oppressive atmosphere of superficiality and cruelness that greeted me daily.

College brought much-needed affirmation and acceptance, but the journey also presented new cases of loneliness. An extended illness my freshman year kept me physically separated from my new friends and classmates. (Thank you, Lord, for my roommate who watched over me!) I met and dated a variety of neat guys, but I started to ache for finding the relationship that would be true for the long haul. Also, the absence of my parents opened up an unexpected type of loneliness for the comfort of their presence, the reassurance when things got bumpy, and their empathy during challenging times; all qualities to which I was accustomed were missing.

God blessed me with this emptiness to show me what my heart was seeking—him. For the first time, I realized how my filling my calendar with activities in order to avoid being alone did not keep him away. He had always been there, ready and willing to keep me company, but I had not made his friendship the very top priority in my life. His stripping away the distractions created the opportunity for me to clearly see what I had only casually acknowledged for so long. I have believed in God since my childhood, but organized "religion" was unable to provide me with an intimate connection to Christ. Therefore, I had not given my faith the commitment Jesus deserved. Though loneliness still pops up here and there, even when I'm with other people, my faith has given me the strength and hope to persevere.

When I started brainstorming for this chapter, my analytical brain immediately began recounting loneliness benchmarks in my past. However, my empathetic brain spoke to me of how Jesus understood my isolation and pain. The analytical side piped up and challenged me to consider just how Jesus related to my suffering; so I did.

Jesus walked the earth completely alone. Yes, he had family, friends, students, and strangers travel with him, but his isolation went far beyond the loneliness attributed to the great and often misunderstood minds in history, to which no one else could possibly relate. Jesus' knowledge and awareness of God, his own role in this world, and the events to come could not be comprehended by any ordinary man or woman. His followers may have believed, but they were not capable of imaging reality through his eyes, heart, and mind. He was the most magnificent, perfect, and amazing teacher, friend, brother, and Savior. Yet he had no peer or true confidant. Only his Father knew his path and his pain.

This new perspective showed me that Jesus, too, had been ostracized, taunted, left alone, and belittled by many. Portrayals of Christ usually depict life moments of working miracles or teaching, not of contemplating loneliness. The mental image of Christ experiencing what I have been though increases my awe of his strength and determination. Over and over again, the Bible tells us to be not afraid, as Christ goes before us in all things. My heart tells me that I will never be and have never actually been alone.

Focus for the Week

Take five minutes each day of this week to focus on loneliness, yours or someone else's. Close your eyes and picture Jesus' arms and spirit wrapped around you, supporting you with his love and compassion. Extend those thoughts into prayers for yourself, family, friends, and strangers that you feel are probably lonely or isolated in the world. Ask for God's grace to comfort those people and bring them friends that are pleasing to him.

Passages

Hebrews 13:5
Luke 9:34–36
Mark 14:32–41

Thanksgiving through Trials

This morning I was still excited about the relaxing and productive day I had yesterday, Monday though it was. Today, after several hours at work, a coworker approached my desk to tell me that one of my bare tires had metal showing and needed to be replaced before it blew out. I thanked her for letting me know and grimaced inside, thinking about the cost of the one, then the cost of all four. Within the hour, I was at home for lunch and noted that our bank account balance was at negative one dollar. I knew that we would have to tap into our equity line to stay afloat. On the way back to work, I opened the mailbox to discover the request for my emissions test and the new tag fees for the year. I sighed. At 5:00 PM, I headed up to the shop where I get my tires and maintenance done, and as I pulled into the lot, my heat gauge went from average to the red zone in a heartbeat. I didn't even want to think about my fading clutch, three oil leaks, and the small part that needed to be replaced under the hood.

So, now I sit in the lobby with a choice. I can wait for the bill in angst and frustration, or I can wait in thanksgiving. I choose the latter.

- Thank you, God, for keeping me safe on tires that have been inadequate for so long.
- Thank you, God, for friends upon whose shoulders your angels sit and whisper observations about my waning tires.
- Thank you, God, for an equity line that seems to be providing so much for us right now when our income is low.
- Thank you, God, that my mechanics will give me six months, same as cash, to figure out how I am going to pay for these hundreds of dollars in parts and services.
- Thank you, God, that my car didn't overheat on the road and in traffic, possibly ruining the engine, causing

an accident, requiring a tow, and forcing me to leave it overnight in someone's shop.
- Thank you, God, that I have transportation of my own, that I may be grateful for simply owning a car that requires fixing.
- Thank you, God, that the arrival of my tag fees and emission notices represent another year of my life in which you have showered me with blessings.
- Thank you, God, for men who go out of their way to work me in at the end of a tiring day or whenever I call, for that matter.

How blessed am I! Thank you, God, for sending me inconveniences that constantly remind me of where I could be without your mercy and grace in helping me along my path. I cannot imagine the sense of being lost that others, who don't know you and your love, experience during such challenging times. May I never stray from the comfort I find in your presence. Thank you, God, for calming my desperation. I know that you will renew my optimistic outlook for the days ahead.

Focus for the Week

Make a list of seven aspects of your life that weigh on your mind negatively. Now go back and find the thanksgiving in each situation or challenge. Try to reframe new experiences that bring you down with hope and newfound appreciation from a different perspective.

Passages

Ephesians 5:20
Psalms 147:7–20

A Message That Gets Lost in Translation

Many people who contemplate becoming churchgoers or official church members often give up on the organized structure. Their reasons vary from lacking time to go to services to a perceived lack of genuine need for God, to not finding Christ's message relevant to their everyday lives. I completely understand these perspectives.

I had a Catholic upbringing, went through many years of classes, was exposed to the sacraments, and learned the appropriate prayers, songs, and rituals. Although I believed in God, his Son, and the Holy Spirit, I lacked a sense of spiritual connection with them. I had no doubt as to the presence of the Trinity, but my heart was not fueled with passion for intimacy with Christ. Consequently, at the age of fourteen, I told my parents that I was no longer attending church. I know that they were disappointed, but I felt like a hypocrite by going to worship without that genuine connection to God. Fortunately, my parents honored my wishes and trusted that my spiritual path was in Jesus' hands. Although God was an integral part of my life, I wanted more than a token relationship, and I knew that the shortcomings were definitely on my end.

Jesus never abandoned me, and he forged a willing and submitting heart in my chest, for which I will always be grateful. However, I was blessed with parents who modeled their very strong faith in Christ from the time I was born. Not all people have loving parents who openly testify and try to live according to the Gospel. Not all people are exposed to the truth of God's perfect sacrifice. Most importantly, not all people are eager to examine their lives and understand why there is only one hope of conquering their sins.

Basically, we are wounded and sinful, and we constantly search for ways to relieve our pain, confusion, and despair. Acknowledging that we lack control of our lives is an intimidating confession. When suffering people seek out a church home, they often are looking for comfort and fulfillment of their current needs. However, depending on the church's style, God's message may seem outdated and miss the point in today's society. Therein lays the problem. God's word is never outdated. His message is timeless, and it relates to each of us every day. Christ came to save the entire world at one time, for eternity. He knew that his parables would be simple enough to carry through thousands of years and still be effective teaching tools for his day. Even the commandments were handed down to Moses in basic terms because God wanted us to clearly understand his laws and grow closer to him.

    We, Christians, need to pray that God will help us *to reach out with words that invite others to come to know him relative to where they are in their own walks of life.* We cannot give up hope that these individuals may receive Christ's message; we must show them that Christ is relevant and necessary to their lives, both today and forever, through our words and by example. As for those who claim not to have time for God or worship, they continue to need our prayers. It's like taking the first step in recovering from an illness or disease. A person has to admit that something is wrong or missing from his life and want to change. Lord, let my prayers encompass those who have not heard your call, and please give me the right words to help your lost children seek out your voice. I will not give up on the nonbelievers, just as you have not given up on your hope for me.

Focus for the Week

Why do some of your family, friends, and acquaintances claim not to believe in the Trinity and/or not attend church or worship services? If you don't know, take this week to ask them. Christ's message can be shared more effectively when you know the history and perspective from which others approach faith or lack thereof. Were they hurt by a church experience? Did they not receive a satisfactory answer to a prayer? Are they disheartened by a life full of struggle and suffering? Remember to consider a person's past when you offer the Gospel to him. People desire relevance with faith. Pray for the right words, that the person listening to your testimony may have ears to hear the truth of God's message, one of love, sacrifice, hope, and compassion.

Passages

John 5:15–47
Luke 4:18–21
Romans 15:18–21

True Confessions

We sin everyday. Man cannot escape his plight, but he possesses hope of Christ's intervention on our behalf and forgiveness of our shortcomings and weaknesses, our selfishness and meanness, and our impatience and ignorance. Yet Christ tells us to not only confess our sins and desire for repentance to him, but he also directs us to speak to one another. This point created fuzziness in my understanding of what the Bible meant by speaking to others. Several churches that I have attended incorporated group or private confessions into their services. Emphasis seemed to be placed on the private and public pronouncement of participants' sinnerhood. These admissions seemed redundant to me, since we, Christians, already know that we are all sinners, and we diligently seek to follow Jesus' ways on the path to forgiveness.

Then I realized that when he spoke of others, perhaps he was guiding us back to the person(s) whom we had hurt or offended in order to ask for their personal forgiveness. Jesus stated that if you forgave other men their sins against you that he would hold them forgiven as well.

A congregation of believers conveys a strong and positive presence in worship, but its acknowledgment of being sinful is not necessary in the process of an individual's confessing his sins and offering reparations to those whom he has offended. Jesus never stated that an intermediary was required in the search for forgiveness from God or man. The only demand God made was to ask human forgiveness from those whom you had hurt before asking for his. Even in the Old Testament, God told men to forego making sacrifices at his altar until each had made peace with anyone against whom he had sinned. This particular instruction demonstrates God's desire for men to forgive each other before they seek his grace.

Asking someone to forgive you doesn't sound like much of a task, but several difficult considerations are required. For instance, you must make yourself vulnerable by being willing to admit fault in a situation. Also, you must display humility and courage in asking for the injured person to reconsider his relationship with you. Furthermore, you must accept the reality that a healing resolution may not occur, though you may be genuinely hopeful that the other person really wants to forgive you. Finally, you must be diligent in guarding your future behavior to prevent that injury from being repeated, whether with your friend or someone else.

Looking back at these steps, I find them quite similar to those that we take in approaching Jesus for forgiveness. However, Christ already knows our true hearts and solemn confessions, and since we *all* sin, the logical conclusion follows that we can never get enough practice in the praying for and the giving of forgiveness. He would probably want us to keep in mind that private injury does not need to be made public, just as demonstration of forgiveness need not be put on display. In some cases, the key lies in three—you, the offended, and God. At other times, you and Jesus can handle your sins. Regardless of the situation, your confessions are personal and confidential, and Christ will do with them what he deems just. No audiences are required.

Focus for the Week

We stumble every day, tripping over our sinnerhood. We count on Jesus to help us walk upright, unworthy though we are. For the next week, focus on controlling your thoughts, words, and deeds. Make them positive and helpful, not negative or judgmental, to yourself and others. When you stumble, speak truthfully to God and ask for his strength to give you the discipline and fortitude to rise above your routine, detrimental habits and casual tendencies. Change your perspective regarding confession and repentance to be exclusively between you and your maker, unless another party has been hurt. If you sincerely seek forgiveness from him, he will know it to be true in your heart and wipe your slate clean.

Passages

James 5:15–16
Psalms 32:1–7

His Invisible Touch

As I've written this book for the Lord, I've become more sensitive to the nuances of my own blessings and the less dramatic, though just as important, characteristics of Jesus' gifts to me. In particular, I am more aware of people's energy, motives, and priorities, as well as opportunities for making decisions. God's invisible touch upon my spirit and to those who have gone through similar experiences seems to clarify questions we might have regarding other individuals, choices, or commitments. For instance, in college my roommate had an unexpected visitor to our apartment. When I greeted the girl at the door, I could feel my skin almost shrink back from her presence. I immediately realized that something was wrong with her energy, though I couldn't pinpoint the cause. I encouraged my roommate to go out with her instead of inviting her into the apartment.

Several days later my boyfriend (who later became my husband) brought his golden retriever over to visit. While he was there, the same girl dropped by to see my roommate. Before I had approached the door, the dog turned to face it and slightly bared his teeth. As I began to open the door, he started to snarl and had to be restrained by my boyfriend. This affirmed to me that God's touch through my intuition had been correct in keeping her out of my home. I have almost never seen a better judge of character than a dog, and Baxter's actions, though startling, made me grateful for listening to my gut instinct.

I believe that God has given us this gift to help protect us from Satan. Just as our conscience is in place to assist us in making healthy decisions, so our intuition can guide and alert us to danger. Our bodies and minds, with a divine spirit, can perceive aggression, hostility, and evil in those around us, though their actions may speak otherwise. I've passed strangers on the street and felt malice in their gaze, manner, and presence. I've seen people on television who were popular, but their spirits seemed less than well-intentioned. I've had acquaintances approach me with hidden agendas and/or lies, and I could tell they were up to no good. I've taken forks in the road that seemed to beckon me one direction, only to discover an accident or crime had occurred simultaneously down the other stretch of highway. I have sometimes heard stories about people who are called off of a plane or convinced not to travel because of the intuition of a loved one or friend, to find out later that a tragedy took place involving that person's planned mode of transportation.

For those who live without Jesus' words and faith, these instances are dubbed random and considered simple coincidence. But we, Christians, know better. God has a purpose for every thought or feeling of which you are capable. How you use or abuse them is completely up to you.

Just as intuition can be used to protect you, so can it also be used to reach out. In the past, my body truly ached around those who seemed to be suffering, though you would never know it by their appearance. My spirit has felt the isolation and loneliness of others, contradicted by their outward social prowess and obvious companionship. It's almost as if their hurting spirits long for healing and comfort from people around them, stretching out in search of anyone who can help them to mend. We need to reach out both physically and prayerfully to these individuals. Why else would God give us the awareness and clarity of their pain?

Lord, I appreciate this invisible gift. Please help me to listen carefully, that it may guide me in a path of safety and one that supports my fellow man in times of need, as another testimony of praise and glory to you.

Focus for the Week

Calm the chaos and craziness surrounding you, so that you can more clearly feel God's touch. Take note of people around you. What does your heart tell you about them that their words and posture don't? Are you drawn to anyone in particular? Why? Open yourself and ask Jesus' spirit to move you according to his will. Let your instincts and availability be at his disposal to reach out to those in need or to protect you from those who would do you harm.

Passages

2 Corinthians 4:1–3
Psalms 40:4–10

What Kind of Student Are You?

Christ is the master teacher. How does your life as a Christian student shape up? I began thinking about my diligence as Jesus' pupil, and I'm afraid I fall short in numerous ways. From day one, my traditional schooling demanded competition of the highest caliber. Yet I distinctly recall that Christ created enough loaves and fishes for all of the multitudes to eat—not just the smartest, strongest, or most motivated of the group. In addition, society feeds the population messages to encourage and reward looking out for oneself; achieving, achieving, and achieving; and not letting anything or anyone stand in your way of self-glorification. However, Jesus specifically instructed us to focus our energy on loving God and fellow neighbors, still another conflict of education. The media glamorizes the path of fame, power, beauty, and seduction that wealth provides for the few. But, Christ clearly tells us in scripture that our true treasures cannot be seen or experienced in this material life; however, we will be showered with them in heaven by serving our Father and his Son.

In today's world, faith can be created to fit any comfort zone or set of beliefs in order to benefit the practitioners on their own terms. Yet Jesus clearly states that the only way to the one, true God is through him, no matter how uncomfortable or inconvenient that seems to nonbelievers. So, while I am concentrating on shutting out the wrong lessons in order to reaffirm the Christ-centered ones, I realize that my daily instruction is just as important.

Am I setting aside private tutoring with Jesus? Am I praising him the same, if not more of the time, than I am making requests for assistance? Am I sharing his Gospel each opportunity I get, as he asks of me? Am I focusing on how he fulfills my needs instead of indulging my wants? Am I modeling Jesus' behavior and teaching by example? Am I seeking his ongoing lessons within scripture? Am I putting time aside to serve others through action and prayer? Am I constantly thanking him for all of his gifts to me, from sunlight to salvation? Am I always humbling myself before him and asking for forgiveness of my sins, that I might be worthy to stand before him in his eternal kingdom?

What would my report card look like were the final school bell to ring for my faith in Christ? I'm sure it would probably read that I "Need Improvement" in a few categories. On second thought, I know it would read that in all of them, since I am unable to be perfect in any area. However, I believe that the overall grade will be determined by the effort, genuine devotion to the spirit, total submission to the teacher, and true humility before the Savior. It is only by eagerly giving of ourselves to Christ that we may receive his final blessing and grace, thereby passing our earthly state and graduating into our spiritual forms for the homecoming celebration of all time.

Focus for the Week

Designate a task for improving your faith each day of the week. Perhaps, the first day you might choose to make reading the Bible a priority. On another day you might decide that practicing humility and asking for forgiveness would enrich your faith. Whatever you choose, remember that faith is not a finite lesson. We must constantly reach and grow with his instruction. There are no shortcuts or cheat sheets in a relationship with Jesus. However, he is more than willing to keep working beside us for as long as it takes.

Passages

1 Corinthians 2:10–16
Mark 4:1–33

God and Dogs

I am such an animal lover. I have been a human parent to twenty-one puppies, eight dogs, two cats, four horses, a fish, three parakeets, a Guinea pig, and foster parented several other canines. Although I had a special place in my heart for each one of them, dogs hold the softest spot. As I lay on the sofa watching my "babies," Ana and Yoshi, relax with full tummies and heavy eyelids, my mind ruminates on the source of my fondness for them. The more I think about them, the more I am reminded of Jesus' qualities in his relationship with me. I find it uncanny how so many parts of my life remind me of my Savior.

Let's take Ana, for example. Regardless of how much time has passed since I last saw her, she is ecstatic to see me. Her little nub and "wiggle-bottom," as my husband and I have named her dancing rear end, cannot be stopped upon my stepping through the front door. I can only imagine how God's heart also elates in our returning home to his love and company. He is just as enthusiastic about the events in my life today as he was when I was a newborn.

Ana constantly watches over me, especially on nights when Bill arrives home late. She monitors the windows, doors, strange sounds from outside, and suspicious squirrel activity in the yard to ensure my safety. God's invisible hand and angels do the same for us, though we often don't see them in action, guiding us through everyday worries or possible dangers. He watches over us every moment of our lives.

My sweet Ana knows when my heart is hurting and will lay her head in my lap, lick my tears, and softly gaze up at me in a manner that says, "I'm sorry. I wish there was something I could do." Christ comforts us through all of our pain and suffering, sometimes while he sits besides us and other times while he is carrying us through the experience. He understands our grieving at the deepest of levels. The pain that he willingly took upon himself kept us from having to ever suffer to the same degree. He generously accepted the most painful path to protect us from it.

Ana "Bo-Bana" is a snuggler and loves to cuddle. Her purr-like sighs of contentment always let me know how much she enjoys my closeness. Her warm, soft fur welcomes me, as does her quiet, gentle breathing. I cannot possibly focus on her and be stressed at the same time. Her presence is soothing to my spirit. Prayer has a similar effect on me. God's grace has calmed me and given me peace during incredibly difficult trials in my life. He has warmed me with his spirit on days when I felt alone and helpless. He gladly took the stress from my shoulders when he knew I couldn't handle it on my own. His support and strength are the pillars that help me to bear the unbearable.

Ana's patience with me never ends. When her dinner hour runs late, she tolerates my doing chores instead of feeding her. The walk I promised yesterday morning might have only materialized last night. My leaving the living room a little bit later than usual to go up to bed finally provides her the prewarmed, coveted sofa spot next to her daddy. So, God willingly and patiently waits for his family, through our business and lack of attentiveness. Though we routinely fail to give him the time and worship of which he is worthy, he continues to joyfully anticipate the next moment when we will spend time together. He attaches no strings or conditions, other than our complete and reverent acceptance of his Son, who fulfilled a promise made to us, for us, in love.

Regardless of what wrong I may have ever done to Ana, her memory of my selfishness is short, and she doesn't hold a grudge. Her forgiveness is pure, without melodrama, pouting, manipulation, or extortion—only love. God has offered us the same relationship. Jesus has already promised us forgiveness of sins. His ultimate sacrifice guaranteed us hope of a clean slate, no matter how grievously we have violated his commandments. We only need to be earnest in our repentance.

Lastly, though most importantly, Ana's love for me is unconditional. She doesn't care about my clothes, the time or place of our togetherness, my bad breath, whether I've showered or remembered her birthday, how much food I have given her, if we've walked or not, how much we have snuggled, or whether she's been for a car ride recently. No matter how hard humans try, this state of love seems beyond our grasp. But, it is God's only form of love. He loves every person, past, present, and future, the same, even with the negative aspects of our decisions. His love dwarfs all of the man-made models that determine if we are worthy of love or not.

Maybe, God blesses us with these wonderful animals to give us a tiny taste of the love that we cannot see or measure—his love. When I examine the similarities between Ana and God, I am certain of one thing. I will spend my entire lifetime trying to become more like Jesus and, consequently, more like my Ana.

Focus for the Week

If you are an animal lover and pet owner, select a trait of your pet that you believe represents an area of your life that needs improvement (i.e., patience, love, enthusiasm). Make this trait a priority for the week. Pretend it is a muscle that requires exercise. Use this exercise to improve yourself and your relationship with Christ by attempting to become more like him. For the nonanimal lovers, select a trait upon which you would like to focus for the week. Even though you lack a furry model, Christ modeled the behavior you have selected to its fullest. Look to him as your guide.

Passages

Corinthians 1:3–10
John 14:23–24

The True Follower

Part of this morning's sermon leapt out at me. What is an ambassador of Christ? The simplicity of the message really struck home, and I have focused on the idea for most of the day. Although the pastor briefly touched upon three basic concepts, I want to examine each to a deeper degree.

First, the true followers of Christ, who desire to lead others to him, do not use his name to further their own agendas. These loyal individuals are not at the forefront of fundraisers making sure that their names are spelled correctly on donation plaques or recognition letters. They do not make a production of pulling checks from their Bibles and showing everyone how much they tithe, how often, or to how many special collection opportunities. They do not erect edifices of splendor to God just to credit themselves. They do not use a claimed faith affiliation to win votes. They do not attend church to be counted present by their fellow man. Their enthusiasm for Jesus' name and their relationship with him is genuine, and their sole motivation is to help others discover the same for themselves.

Second, these ambassadors have nothing to hide. This does not mean that their lives are flawless or even inspiring. Simply put, they have owned up to their sins and shortcomings with Christ. He is their only judge, and their relationship with him and personal everyday struggles with sin are open for everyone to witness. However, through their hope and thankfulness for redemption, their eagerness for others to seek and find Jesus never wanes.

Third, promoters of faith in Christ have nothing to lose. All that they have, they know God has provided them, most importantly the offer of eternal life. Were Christ to strip away their material wealth, physical health, and the comfort of loved ones, the basis of their faith would remain. Ambassadors do not judge their lives via the superficial trappings of society. These things can vanish in a second. However, God was here long before any of said blessings had been given, and he will remain after they are no longer needed.

The difference for some is that when these simple things are stripped away will they have anything left? For the followers of Christ, hope will continue to resonate. For others, they may believe that they are truly lost. Fortunately, it's never too late to discover Jesus' presence and necessity in your life. An ambassador of Christ trusts that Jesus will provide everything crucial to a follower's path and the spreading of his message. His faithfulness to us will never waver, and loyal followers yearn to lead others to that revelation. Lord, help me find a way to lead the lost to you.

Focus for the Week

If you broke your faith down into parts, how many of those parts, if any, resemble a true follower's path? Do you recognize any of these three qualities of ambassadorship for Christ in yourself? In people you know? Are the qualities you see the positive traits that magnify Jesus' glory, or do they turn away from him? Use this week to practice being a guide to help those who are wandering aimlessly find Christ. Jesus perfectly demonstrated how to live a life that honored his Father, and he continued to try and witness to the common man, politicians, and lawmakers of the time, though most would not listen. Pray for discernment and wisdom, that you can easily identify those who are wandering and offer them Christ's Gospel. Beware those whose narcissistic agendas go against the Almighty. Keep your focus on Jesus and help those around you to do the same.

Passages

2 Corinthians 5:20–6:11
Matthew 6:1–21

Under Attack

During the last week or so, as I have picked up the pace on my book, I have been under an active attack from Satan. Sleep has escaped me for about five nights, and the other nights provided only a few hours of rest here and there. My dreams have been horribly terrifying, twisted, and evil. They have resulted in multiple panic attacks each night, which is unusually high, compared to one attack monthly over the past year. Completely exhausted by the weekend, I was so lethargic and unmotivated to do anything, especially to work or write. Every task quickly became a chore, and I realized how essential fitful sleep is to my everyday life. My fatigue makes me vulnerable to Satan's attempts to sabotage my life and faith. He will exploit my weaknesses to their fullest, making focusing a challenge for any period of time, thereby making focused prayer even more difficult. The more of this book I complete, the more I find obstacles popping up in my path to knock me back, discourage my efforts, or cast doubt on God's journey with me. This pattern motivates me to charge ahead and finish, since I know that this book will keep me rooted to what is important in my life—spending time thinking about, praying to, thanking, and praising Christ's name.

We are all under attack in every time and place. Satan uses stress, insomnia, illness, grief, anger, loss, and other daily experiences to try and destroy our connection to our Father. His bold attempt to ruin that relationship was perfectly demonstrated when he confronted and tried to manipulate Jesus face-to-face. Christians accept that suffering is part of life, but we must hold steadfast to our faith, especially during the times that hurt the most. People often look for lessons in their misery; I feel like the lesson is not in the "what" that is going on, but in the "how" we process it in our relationship with God. If you consider that our sole purpose for being created is to worship Christ and be loved by him, then Satan has an infinite list of strategies for driving wedges between our Savior and us.

Losing a loved one is devastating. Frequently, those left behind ache, cry, don't eat, can't sleep, scream, and withdraw from everyone. I know that Satan thrives on the pain and mixed emotions that rise up during such a time. He revels in the anger and hostility that the grieving may have toward God. Confusion, a sense of being lost, and general lack of understanding (why me?) are angles of weakness upon which Satan preys. Any door opened through doubt or frustration offers him another opportunity to insert a division into your intimate relationship with Jesus.

This is why struggling to maintain and strengthen your faith is so crucial. Do you truly believe that God demands a content follower all of the time? Did Christ tell us that we should come to him, but only when things are going great in our lives? No! Why do you think his suffering was so essential to our salvation? He wants you to know that there is nothing you can say or do in your grief and pain that will make him love you any less. He wants you to believe that his arms are around you from beginning to end. He asks you to trust that his vision for your life is best, though it may be in conflict with your personal plans. He desires for you to cling to his Gospel and promises, no matter how much easier it may seem to loosen your diligence in prayer and worship during painful times. He knows your suffering and is willing to share the path of healing with you. On the other hand, Satan is only interested in blurring and cluttering the way with isolation, resentment, and depression.

We are under attack every moment. My family, friends, and acquaintances are coping with serious illnesses, financial crises, relationship woes, family wounds, professional criticisms, transitions, layoffs, and experiences that test their faith at every turn. Christ uses these times as outreach opportunities for his family. Challenges are catalysts for spiritual growth, and the more we lean on Jesus to carry us through the desperation and impossible pain, the closer to him we become.

We are under attack, so arm yourself with the protection that only God can offer. Know that you are attacked because you are loved and cherished by the Almighty. Know that your life and how you live it has value and potential beyond measure. Know that you are under attack, but also know that you are a warrior of God's army. You are fighting the battles each day, but Jesus has already won the war. Know it, put on the armor of God, and be strong and grateful for his protection.

Focus for the Week

In what ways do you feel like Satan may be trying to create distress in your life? How do you respond to his attacks? Do you struggle with the stress, trying to conquer his aggression by yourself, or do you turn to the Lord for his courage, wisdom, and perseverance through the trial? What better defense could you have against evil than the Savior who will one day have his ultimate vengeance on Satan and his followers? Don't let these challenging events distance you from God. You will be in the palm of his hand, regardless of whether you remain on speaking terms or not. His love for you never wavers, so don't let your faith and trust in him falter. Hold up your shield of faith and let it protect you from Satan's attacks.

Passages

Ephesians 6:10–17 (armor of God)
Matthew 4:1–11

Jesus, the Universal Language

Thousands of years ago, the chosen people of God, who were descendents of Noah, decided to build a tower to reach up to heaven. Their numbers were great, and their egos were such that they believed, through their own efforts and creativity, that any feat could be accomplished. As their tower grew, so their arrogance expanded with it. God watched and was displeased with their attitudes and actions. His consequence for this behavior was to scatter them into many separate nations across the Earth. He did not use the threat of battle with an enemy or drought and famine to cause this upheaval. Instead, he utilized the tool upon which they relied heavily, their ability to communicate with one another through language. God made each mouth and ear foreign to the words and sounds around them. The people became frustrated and lost, so they left to find new lands and those with whom they could live. The tower, itself, was named the Tower of Babel based on the Lord's judgment on his people. Those who had worked so hard to reach God's domain were left to only babble at one another, without comprehension of or satisfaction in the mutual achievement of the structure.

Once mankind had spread to all corners of the world, how would God choose to unite them again? In his infinite wisdom, he sent the ultimate vessel, his Son. Jesus is our universal language; all can know him if their hearts desire it to be so. Jesus always spoke simply, and his messages were concise and clear. His relationships with his fellow man were not based on their wealth, power, level of education, location, or affiliation. Easily understanding his Good News, truth, and purpose came naturally for those who placed their lives in Christ's hands. Once again, man was given the ability to become united.

Unfortunately, not everyone is interested in the Gospel and the truth it represents. Although this can be frustrating for Christians, the Bible tells us that there will be those who remain lost from God's word until the end of days. God's voice will not compete with people whose minds are filled with narcissistic agendas and priorities. The clutter of selfishness is sure to guarantee deafness and distraction from our Father's gentle and tender tones. We, believers, should continue to rejoice in the blessing of language that we have been given in Christ. For one day we will hear the most beautiful syllables from our Father and his Son, as we look upon their countenances of glory. Only then will we be able to fully celebrate the pureness of God's language and the privilege of having been selected to hear, understand, and rejoice in the meaning of it.

Focus for the Week

Is God's presence obvious to you? If not, how do you think you might have dismissed his attempts to reach you? What can you do to make sure you don't miss his words in the future? If so, were you alone or with a group? Did the experience occur at a church function, during a vacation, or simply while you were moving through your day? Did a specific or profound event bring you to Christ? Was your motivation out of need or desire to know him? Make this week's mission to study God's word, both through scripture and prayer. Read the words that others heard from Jesus and his Father and the instructions, lessons, and wisdom that they offered. Share these messages with those around you, whether with family, friends, a church group, or a stranger.

Passages

Ephesians 4:13–32
Genesis 11:1–9

Completely Obedient

This morning on my way to work, I drove through my first shower of falling autumn leaves. The childlike thrill came from my lips in a small "yippee," and I scanned the road ahead for any other possible leaf shower activity through which I could steer. Tonight, as I sit and pray for God's will in my pen, the changing foliage strikes a thought. God's creations have different levels of obedience to his teachings and instructions. The weather, plant life, and abysses of ocean and space give no resistance to his will. Every pine needle clings to its tree until he wishes it let go. Each ripple on the sea washes ashore in his time. Stars shine and collapse as fits his judgment. Clouds form and shift with his very breath.

Though the animals of our world have minds of their own, they are simply driven by their God-given instincts for survival, feelings that help them to stay alive and multiply and unknowingly provide resources for mankind. Although these species have intelligence, an awareness of their creator is not apparent in their behavior. Following animals, we have man—the self-appointed, most intelligent form of life on this planet. Yet man, with all of his abilities, IQ, experience, and freedom of thought, has distanced himself further from God than any other form of life on Earth. Though God personally sacrificed a living part of himself so that he could save his incredible creation from their sin, humans consciously and arrogantly fill their days with indulgence instead of gratitude and self-righteousness instead of humility. We consider ourselves to be extremely advanced beings. Yet our behavior defies the very being in whose image we were formed. Man continues to choose lifestyles and priorities that not only disregard or disrespect our Father, but these choices also often represent the glorification of sin.

If tides submit to his hand, day and night, surely we can focus on giving our attention and will over to his direction and love. Scripture states that a day will come when all of God's creations will sing out to Christ. As we work on our own obedience to our Savior, perhaps we should be warming up our voices. Let us be ready to join the eager choruses, whether they are plants, animals, or heavenly hosts.

Help me, Lord, to find celebration in my total submission to you, knowing that my only happiness comes directly from your spirit. Move and mold me, Lord, in ways that are pleasing to you. Use me, oh God, to do your will completely. Protect me with your spirit, angels, and armor, that I may have the strength to deny the lures of sin. Forgive me for the times when I have been weak and failed. Leave no hair on my head, thought in my mind, or feeling of my heart untouched by the desire to obey your calling.

Focus for the Week

How would you gauge your level of obedience to Jesus? Is it "only when convenient"? During the course of this week, acknowledge the lack of obedience in your daily life and ask God for his forgiveness. Make obedience a top priority on your spiritual journey with God. If you are aware of times when you stumble and fall short, ask Christ to help you walk upright again. The greatest blessing of free will is the opportunity to choose his will over our own.

Passages

Acts 5:27–32
Deuteronomy 11:22–28

Moths Don't Know Any Better

Have you ever stood underneath a street lamp or porch light at night and watched the circling insects in the bulb's glow? This phenomenon fascinates me, and I enjoy bearing witness to the assortment of animal life drawn out of the darkness. I, myself, love light—sunlight, moonlight, firelight, floodlights, interior "décor" lights, and especially candlelight. I am drawn to the light for many of the same reasons that I am drawn to Christ. Light expels all darkness around it. The two cannot occupy space simultaneously. Even a tiny candle can dispel blackness so much greater than itself, thereby giving those nearby a sense of safety. Jesus does the same with the darkness in my life—fear, doubt, insecurity, and feelings of inadequacy. He erases them with his presence, showing me what he sees in me—potential, hope, and love. His light also provides me with comfort and security, allowing me to see the truth of what lies around me and keeping me from fearing the unknown. Most light produces warmth. I place myself in beams of sunlight whenever possible, soaking it in through every pore. Inside I huddle over candles, cupping my hands over the flickering flame and lowering my face to the heat. Christ is the same with my soul. He draws me near to him, warming me up when I grow distant and cold and keeping me safely in his hand.

Light is essential for the growth of the majority of plant life on the planet. Not only do plants and animals require sunlight, but humans also gain necessary nutrients from it as well. So, Jesus feeds our souls with his light. Without his light, we would be unable to spiritually grow and develop. His light goes beyond sustaining us; he shines it upon us that we may thrive and flourish in the acceptance of his love.

Even if every light source could be combined into one, humongous beam, that light falls short when compared to Christ. He *is* the light of the world. Every need we have, he will satisfy. Without the radiance of his glory, we are lost. Lord, please help me to remember the passion of your spirit, the eternal flame, the light of my salvation. Let it shine upon me, within me, and through me, that I may help others to come out of the blackness and cold in your name. Thank you for shielding me from the ever-present darkness in the world. Let it fear my confidence in you and your light.

Focus for the Week

Find a quiet time to sit in a dark room and light a candle. Use this time to reflect, pray, share your day with Jesus, or give thanks for your blessings. Enjoy the light, its warmth, and how it reaches throughout the room. Note how the flame influences how you are feeling, both inside and out. When outdoors, soak up the sun's rays and consider its role in so much plant growth around you. Imagine how much greater Christ's light is than the sun, and his light will never go out.

Passages

John 1:1–17, 7:12
Revelation 21:23

The Altar of God

Bill and I were headed to see my parents in North Carolina. In addition to listening to the '80s hits blaring from the radio, hanging our heads out the window with the dogs to savor the mountain air, and stopping for snacks and bathroom breaks, we enjoyed reading scripture, though for only short periods of time to avoid motion sickness. I vividly recall opening my Bible to Exodus and starting to read at the twentieth chapter. The conversation is between God and Moses regarding the Ten Commandments.

We had been through this passage many times through church services, independent readings, and discussions with fellow Christians. However, this particular afternoon's recitation revealed something I hadn't noticed before that day. *God keeps talking* to Moses after he has given the original commandments to him. With a majority of churches, all of the focus is placed on the first ten instructions, and nothing is said about the rest of the conversation. The discussion relates to three additional points. First, God discusses how to make an altar of earth for the sacrifices. Since Christ provided himself as the perfect sacrifice, we no longer need to appease God with animal sacrifices, so this process is no longer necessary. Second, he describes how an altar of stone should be made, if Moses chose to do so, by using a stone that has not been hewn or cut with any kind of tool, since this would have polluted the stone. However, God's last words were the ones that truly caught my attention. "Neither shalt thou go up by steps unto mine altar, that thy nakedness be not discovered thereon" (Exod. 20:26).

God's own words demanded that man in the Old Testament not go up stairs onto his altar. Only the individuals whom God designated were worthy to approach the altar and present sacrifices for the atonement of the people. Otherwise, they would have realized their degree of sinfulness and lacking in God's eyes, which would have been incredibly painful and humiliating. When Jesus sacrificed himself, he atoned for every man's sins forever; therefore, we may all approach his altar and worship freely and without fear.

The verse from Exodus 20:26 drew my attention because it reminded me of another conflict between some Christian leaders (teachers, ministers, etc.) and Jesus. Often, when he taught, Christ was among the people, standing at their level or sitting on the ground, perhaps even moving to the top of a hillside for better exposure to the masses. Even though he had every right to elevate himself, he chose to meet them eye-to-eye. I think he wanted to emphasize that he lived with them and for them, not above them. However, some modern-day Christian leaders use altars to elevate themselves above those who have entrusted their spiritual guidance and development to them. Now the altar that was originally built to honor God has become more of a stage in some churches. Instead of honoring Jesus by respecting the sanctity of the altar, various men have made worship more into a show of rituals, empty promises, and self-glorifying proclamations.

Perhaps, others would disagree, but I have always felt like no man should be elevated above any other, whether by status or by simple, physical proximity. Only one man exists whose words and teachings are above us all—Jesus Christ. An altar is a holy and sacred place. Many types of instructors stand upon platforms and stages in order to be seen and heard by many, but those edifices are not dedicated to our Lord. Those teachers are sought out because of the academia they have to offer, not for spiritual nurturing, strengthening, and guidance. Seek out spiritual leaders whose egos are grounded in humility and passion for Christ. Beware of those who eagerly climb the altar steps each week to find their place in the spotlight. Rejoice in knowing that Jesus has called us all to approach his altar to accept his forgiveness and grace. Search for others whose enthusiasm for Christ is contagious. Celebrate his invitation side-by-side with your spiritual family, but make sure that Jesus is the one to whom you lift your eyes and heart.

Bill and I must have driven sixty miles just talking about this passage. I was grateful for having flipped to it, since I had obviously missed a few, crucial details in my studies. I mention these verses because they prove that I'd been overlooking significant information for many years, though I was very familiar with the preceding verses. I have since learned to become more thorough in my Bible study. I've started reading aloud, since I remember his word better when I hear it. Verbalizing his message also slows me down and keeps me from skimming or skipping words and phrases here and there. I have to actively focus on each word and thought. I now absorb more of his message, which hopefully means I am missing fewer of those previously overlooked passages. Keep your eyes open for those overlooked details. Ignorance is no excuse, and I say that from much experience.

Focus for the Week

Use this week to experiment with different ways to experience God's word. Try reading it aloud, if you don't already. If you read aloud, try studying with a family member or friend and have him or her read. You listen, instead. If you have used both of these techniques, write a short sentence or two summarizing each chapter you have read. If you have other ideas, give them a try.

Passage

Exodus 20

A Blessing by Choice

Are you genuinely satisfied? For me satisfaction comes from different times, sources, and places. I recall incredible meals that ended with everyone gathering around a fire for long talks and relaxation. I remember physically demanding projects that took hours, days, or weeks to complete. I see past images of moments when I received high marks or praise for efforts extended to accomplish school or work-related tasks. My senses return me to quiet snuggles and naps with my dogs at various stages of their lives, when our breathing and contentedness blended together to make a pile of laziness and dreaming. I picture the times when my face has been nuzzled in my husband's warm neck, his arms around me, and my eyes closed, soaking in the simplicity of a hug and silent moment of sharing.

The common theme between these moments is that they represented times of peace and satisfaction in my life. In addition, God provided them for my happiness. Each event seemed to quell any stressors or items on my "do" or "worry" lists, even if only for a short while.

So, why are these times the exception instead of the rule? Satisfaction is a blessing of our own choosing. To be content with your life is to tell God that you are grateful and fulfilled by his generosity. Imagine that you are a parent and your days are consumed by your child's constant wishes, demands, pleas, and discontentedness, though you have loved, fed, bathed, clothed, sheltered, educated, protected, counseled, and disciplined him. In neglecting to recognize or appreciate what you have provided, your child seems to be missing out on his blessings or taking them for granted. Perhaps, if everyone tossed out their "want" list and praised Jesus for our "already-been-given" list, we could grow to be satisfied with the entirety of our lives, not just with isolated moments or experiences.

Now imagine that same child telling you that he has enjoyed his life of privilege and love and he trusts you to take care of the details. What better demonstration of faith and graciousness could we possibly extend to our own Father? Christ did not wander through his life with fear or resignation that God might fail to provide for his needs. Neither should we. Jesus was satisfied. He lived in each moment, soaking in his opportunities to serve, give, and teach. Please, Lord, help me to strive for daily satisfaction. Let me be a reminder, for others and myself, that you have given us more than we could ever possibly come by on our own. My cup overflows—always. Let me not dwell on the gifts washing over the rim, but let me focus on the ones inside, for I know that you will never stop pouring.

Focus for the Week

Choose one day of the upcoming week, and instead of using it to sort through your list of requests, make your mission to identify and be grateful for your blessings. Let your reflection include the big and the small blessings. The length of your list might surprise you. Let your satisfaction be felt in your heart, that Jesus might be glorified in your contentedness.

Passages

Ecclesiastes 1:8
Hebrews 13:5–6

The Ability to Say No

Using the model of perfect generosity and compassion as our guide, Christians often adopt the attitude and philosophy of the "yes" life, saying "yes" to any opportunity for giving that they can. This is quite admirable and benefits many people in countless ways, but I have also seen numerous people who have not only exhausted themselves by saying "yes" to everything, but who have also physically made themselves sick, as well as damaged their close, personal relationships.

Christ desires genuine giving from all men, but he has also stated that he wishes happiness for his family. For some, giving provides just that—satisfaction and contentment. However, balance is important in preserving one's physical, emotional, and spiritual health while giving. God commanded us to love our neighbors as we love ourselves. By this he expresses that we treat our neighbors *the same as* we would treat ourselves—no better, no worse. This does not mean that we need to go without sleep, food, or recreation in order to constantly serve others' needs. The individuals doing the giving must take time to recharge their own spiritual, emotional, and physical batteries before being able to passionately assist others. God wants us to enjoy our own blessings as much as we enjoy sharing them. This requires developing the ability to say "no."

Instead of trying to be in on every committee, fundraising effort, service project, and church function, select a few and focus your energy on them. Remember, it's quality, not quantity, that matters. Learn how to take time for yourself that is not already filled with obligations or volunteer commitments. Feel comfortable with telling family members and friends that you need time for rest and relaxation, either solo or with your spouse. Leave the familiar, self-embraced, guilty feelings in the past. Resist the temptation to fill every empty position yourself. Keep in mind that God may be waiting for someone else to grow through a position that you are eyeing. If you fill all of them, what does that leave for the rest of the group?

In a way we are all here to support Christ's group project. Each of us has our gifts, talents, and generosity to contribute, but not all in the same place, time, or fashion. The key is that we do not rely on others to fill the positions and opportunities that God intended for us. He will show us where he wants us, if we pray and pay attention.

Focus for the Week

Make yourself the priority this week. Search for the strength and confidence to say "no" to a request that prevents you from taking time to nurture yourself, whether with sleep, a satisfying book, exercise, or a hobby. Understand that you must practice this response, especially if you are out to try and save the world at every turn. That's God's job, and Christ has already done this for you. So you can relax. He wants you to be healthy and happy, and learning to take care of yourself will always benefit others more than if you are run-down, sick, and frustrated.

Passages

Luke 10:38–42
Romans 15:2–5

His Timing

Today, I will do absolutely nothing productive. For the last several weeks, Bill and I have tried our best to prepare our house for selling. We have been juggling the long list of fix-up tasks, our full-time jobs, and Yoshi's need for constant supervision, medication, and physical rehabilitation from his spinal surgery. Yesterday, my gas tank of energy and patience hit empty. I felt like the world was hurling projects and events at us at such a frenzied pace that we had more to do in less time—every day. The revelation struck as I stood at the base of our deck stairs staining the tiny, inner slats, a chore much too tedious for late in the afternoon. I knew that this job could not be physically completed in the time we had allotted, compliments of nasty weather and waning hours of daylight after work. The more clutter we put away, the more I found it elsewhere—or it found me. Finishing one task only revealed the need to address another.

Then last night we met with a dear friend, who is helping us to market our home. He has watched over us for the last seven years, and his experienced eye as a realtor is a fantastic asset. His list of recommendations was short, but expensive, so we quickly decided what we would need to tackle ourselves and what had to be professionally done. Afterward, he gently presented the comparable homes in our neighborhood and shared that he thought our asking price might be too high. This compounded our frustration, since we were still searching for another home into which to move. We were counting on every bit of our home's equity to help us recover from the last two years of tremendous financial challenge.

I thought back to the night that our friend and I had first looked at this very house. We agreed that it would be the last (of an extremely, lengthy list) for at least three months, since we had exhausted the available homes in the area. We know that Christ brought us into this house seven years ago, and he provided us with an opportunity to get through these challenging times long before we ever saw them coming. With God, surprises are the rule, not the exception. So, when he says "wait," we listen.

Hence, my new list of priorities takes over this morning. I plan to pay particular attention to many nonwork-related tasks today, including snuggling with my puppies, napping, snacking, enjoying TV "veg" time, writing, more napping, reading, walking, and possibly going on a date with that handsome man who lives in our house but whom I rarely see. In honor of my trust in Jesus, I will give my patience a rest and my body a break. I will also pray that he will assist me in keeping perspective and peace at the center of our plans, since they are always subject to change without notice. His timing is perfect; it's mine that requires ongoing adjustment. Therefore, we will continue to work on the projects we can, and we will trust that when the time is right God will have us out of our home and into a new one that is pleasing to him. We continue to believe that he will also provide us with much needed rest.

Focus for the Week

Think of an aspect of your life that causes you to be impatient. What is it about this part of your life that is so frustrating? Use this week to make a concerted effort to cope with this issue in a positive way. Change how you view it and the importance you place upon it so that you don't experience as much stress in the future. Ask God to give you a coping strategy or to carry this concern for you.

Passages

Isaiah 30:18–21
Lamentations 3:22–26

Christmas Traditions

As a child I loved to soak every ounce of Christmas festivities and traditions into my pores. I enjoyed hanging the greenery on our front porch, dipping chocolate-covered pretzels, unpacking and assembling our family's nativity scenes, and decorating the tree. Our "possum pine" came from neighbors' fields, and they could only be acquired on the coldest of days in the heart of knee-high briars and crowded thickets. The tree lights became my designated duty after years of my mom losing patience with the tangled wires and burned-out segments on each string. We were blessed in my dad's years of exhaustive effort and long work hours that provided us with material comfort and holiday festivities, but most of my fondest memories came from our time spent visiting with loved ones and serving the needy over the holiday season.

When I got married, Bill and I had to decide which traditions to continue and which to leave behind in place of our own. After several years of ambivalence and procrastination, he finally asked me why I chose to celebrate Christmas in certain ways. I told him that it was because these traditions were accepted and practiced by many generations of my family and by a large part of society, some of whom aren't even Christians, and I had come to really enjoy them. He said that when it comes to my faith, doing something because "it's always been done this way," doesn't suffice. I agreed, and he encouraged me to research my traditions before we made our final choices.

I prepared myself for the idea that my list might be slightly shortened by my research, but I was mistaken. The results of what I discovered astounded me. I realized that I needed to examine more clearly how I celebrate my Savior, both at Christmas and at other times during the year, instead of continuing the rituals with which I had become comfortable and known for so long.

The first piece of history I uncovered related to the selection of December 25 as the designated date of celebration. According to a variety of sources, this day was selected by the church in an attempt to counteract the pagan festival of

Saturnalia, which included everything from heavy partying and drinking (and sometimes nudity) in the streets to animal sacrifices and idol worship.[1-3] The timing had little to do with Christ's actual birth, which historians date back to the fall season, since Joseph and Mary had to travel back to Joseph's home to be counted for the census (tax time).

Next under the microscope went the Three Wise Men. These men did not journey to find Jesus in order to celebrate his birth. They were sent by Herod to pinpoint the child's location and determine if he was truly a threat to Herod (i.e., needed to be killed). The gifts they gave him were simply the goods they had with them at the time. When their eyes were opened and they realized he was actually the Son of God, they worshipped him and later took different routes back to their homes, trying to avoid Herod and his questions. God had moved in their hearts and minds, changing them from the politicians in Herod's pocket to men who fell on their knees before the world's King of Kings.

From there I moved on to the Christmas tree. I discovered this decoration to have its origin with Nordic traditions (dating back to the twelfth century) which were based on celebrating the passing of the winter solstice, one of the coldest and harshest times of year. Families would chop down, decorate, sometimes anoint, and burn the tree, or Yule log, to one of their gods. It usually burned for about twelve days and provided them with warmth and a source by which they could prepare food. This period of time was filled with celebration and feasting to honor the Nordic god of the (winter) sun, Jolnir (also Odin). Families also believed that this ritual would protect them from witchcraft, dispel evil spirits from their homes, and bring them luck.[2]

Santa was next on my list. The jolly, old elf has an interesting background. His image was very loosely modeled after Bishop Nicholas of Myra, Turkey, around 310 AD.[3] Though most of his history may be more legend than fact, stories have been passed from age to age and from European countries to others around the world regarding him as a miracle-working Christian who looked after children and sailors and was referred to by a variety of names. Eventually, he was designated Saint Nicholas and had churches and holidays dedicated in his honor. Some followers actually prayed to and worshipped him. As time passed, his name and image were changed by many artists and countries who added different types of clothing, accessories, and story lines, including "A Visit from St. Nicholas" which eventually became "The Night Before Christmas." Now he is surrounded with flying animals, a magic sleigh, and elf helpers. Although his alleged beginnings were steeped in generosity and kindness, the metamorphosis of his image and the consequent commercial frenzy that have evolved have steamrolled over his original message of devotion to Christ. Instead of a picture of a loving, gift-giving, humble gentleman, his warped image has become one of materialism that encourages children to line up with a list of things that they want and have come to expect each December. The truth is that Santa was originally modeled after a man who used his life to honor Jesus. That man, his image, and his values are now vague and distant shadows of many centuries passed, at least in the United States.

Becoming even more frustrated after diving into mistletoe (a pagan symbol for fertility) and other traditional Christmas decorations, I turned back to my Bible for guidance. I actively sought out God's wishes for the celebration of Jesus' birth. I found very little about decoration and plenty about adoration.

The only Christmas tree reference I could find was in Jeremiah (chapter 10). One verse specifically and clearly states that it is a heathen practice to cut down a tree, bring it inside, decorate it, and nail it to the floor. I found the wording quite startling, considering that the prophet Jeremiah wrote these words before Christ was even born.

I failed to find anything in the Bible regarding the rest of these points. Although I searched for scriptural guides to proper celebrations, I found none directed toward Jesus' birthday. I ended up falling back on Christ's own words and priorities. He remained focused on two things during his life and openly stated their importance: loving his Father and loving his earthly family. So, I told Bill that I wished to do the same. I wanted to honor Jesus in a manner that was free of pagan rituals, symbols, and figureheads and only included him. Therefore, we packed up all of our ornaments and decorations, opting for a few white strings of lights above our kitchen cabinets for cozy lighting and the feeling of warmth and as many candles as were affordable, scattered throughout the house as a reminder of Jesus' light for the world. We also wanted to continue serving the needy each holiday season with my parents and sister, as well as whenever possible during the year. After spending so much time searching for ways to express our enthusiasm and gratefulness for Christ's arrival, I felt that sharing our blessings and love would be the greatest way to honor the one who bestowed every ounce of grace and privilege upon us.

I will miss the traditions that I enjoyed with my family and the pleasure we took with them, and I will treasure those memories forever. Yes, when family and friends now come over during the holidays, they seem concerned with our lack of "Christmas" décor and ask why we don't celebrate. We try to avoid any awkwardness by treating the lack of ornaments very matter-of-factly, though I sometimes feel like others don't understand that lack of decoration doesn't represent a lack of celebration. That's okay with us. We simply don't want to offend our Lord by using irreverent tokens and objects to praise the season of his birth (whenever it may have occurred), only to one day stand before him and have to explain how tradition and rituals overrode our passion and intentions.

In a way, we have surrounded ourselves with material things that distract us from his presence, through decorations, stories, and gifts. All he desires is our love, attention, and devotion and our reaching out to others as he did to us. He brought the only important and necessary gift. Why are we so busy adopting and creating these other things?

Focus for the Week

Celebrate Christ's birth every day; value each day the same. Celebrate in a fashion that you believe is pleasing to him. Research the forms of celebration and decoration to ensure that they do not blaspheme his name or go against scripture. The intentions of most individuals at this time of year are kind and generous; however, our society has incorporated rituals and symbols that go against God since they originated from groups that worshipped other gods. We cannot let our ignorance of traditions be an excuse for offending our Lord. Be active and educated in your pursuit of praising his name and giving thanks for his birth.

Passages

Jeremiah 10
Luke 2:7–21
Matthew 1:18–25

Hypocrite or Not?

To be human is to be a hypocrite. Man consistently contradicts himself by saying one thing and doing another. Jesus never had this problem, since he always spoke truthfully, shared openly, and followed God's teachings and laws perfectly. He had no hidden agenda and demonstrated strength in the execution of his will.

Today, various nonchurchgoers and even Christians condemn organized Christianity as being hypocritical. They claim that some Christians pretend to be something they aren't. These critics believe that followers of Jesus should demonstrate their faith though action instead of simply talking about it. I suppose that they expect model Christians to spring forth from churches as proof of true Christianity's fruit.

I can relate to their perspective and feelings. For instance, I admit that I have attended worship services with people who seemed to be going through the motions. I used to be one of them. I have witnessed individuals who lived one way during the week and another way on Sundays. I, too, used to wonder "what's the point," when watching others keeping up the apparent facades of religious routines.

The truth is that we are *all* hypocrites, though maybe not every moment or about the same things. Christ offers us a way to repent of this human flaw. He sees how we are constantly torn between what we know and say is the right choice and other options that create hypocrisy and encourage fickleness in our decision-making. Humbly owning up to this unattractive quality provides us the first tool toward battling it. In addition, Christ and his church body provide reminders of our fallibility and sinfulness while simultaneously praying for our continued strength, courage, and faith in trying to eliminate the hypocrisy in our lives. We continue to be works in progress, which also makes us vulnerable to sin and poor choices. God has promised us his love and support with our struggle with both.

So, yes, you will find hypocrites in every church, just as frequently as you will discover them on the streets or in the media.

If this is the case, why do we hear such harsh criticism about *Christian* hypocrites? Perhaps, those looking in expect to see greater effort and better behavior from Christians, which is logical, considering that good works follow naturally from those who have claimed Jesus as their Savior. Maybe, some are searching for a church that appears less hypocritical in nature because they've recognized their own need for healing and repentance and are seeking a confident congregation that will help them conquer their personal challenges. Perhaps, familiarity with members of the church community is important to them. Others might need to join a spiritual body that pushes their faith to a higher level.

Regardless of the reason that these people are examining church homes, they must remember two key elements in their selection. First, no church is hypocrite-free. Second, Jesus is the only one who can truly help us in conquering our sinful nature and actions. Genuine fellowship with other Christians can only be experienced by acknowledging God's saving grace and being vigilant in holding ourselves accountable in relationships with our fellow man. Even though a man's actions may not reflect this diligence, the absence of obvious fruit does not necessarily mean that he is failing in his struggle to be a Christian. Each man is on his own spiritual path, no two the same in timing and development. The people you see around you may have already come a long way in God's eyes, though you might judge them as lacking. In the same context, a church congregation can offer prayer and encouragement, but the crucial aspect of one's presence in a church body should be based on what a person brings before God, in praise, accountability, and repentance, not how someone compares himself to the other church members.

Hypocrisy is what happens when we spend too much time worrying about the judgments of those around us and not enough attention to the one within us. Christ provided us a model with his life, but he knows that we are incapable of reaching the high standard that he set, at least if we rely solely on ourselves. He will judge each man, not by his works (whether empty or fruitful), but by his heart (the true measure of a man's faith).

Jesus uses our hypocrisy and our other shortcomings as fertilizer for our souls. From them, opportunities for spiritual growth and fortification sprout and may prosper. Our attempts to overcome the constant barrage of temptation and sinful lures will result in glorifying Christ through the sweet and savory fruit that we will naturally bear. These deeds flow from God's love through us, not as actions that originate in our own minds. Christians cannot please Jesus by making a checklist of activities that they believe will make him happy. His pleasure comes from our love for him and our faith in him. Our consequent thoughts and actions happen innately, demonstrating our compassion for our fellow man and further proclaiming Christ's majesty.

Lord, may the fruits of our love for you be testimony to the hope that you have offered all men, even though we remain hypocrites.

Focus for the Week

Examine your hypocrisy and that of those around you. How can you improve your relationship with Jesus so that your actions reflect more fruit instead of sin? Although we cannot change others, is there some aspect of your life that you could change for the better that might provide a more positive model of behavior for someone you know who has difficulty with hypocrisy? Focus on saying what you mean and doing what you say this week. Most importantly, contemplate your relationship with Christ before saying or doing anything that might draw you closer to a sinful thought or deed.

Passages

Luke 13:10–17
Matthew 23:1–39

The Supreme Divider

I have been taught to refer to Jesus as "The Prince of Peace," "The Lamb," and "Savior." The images by which my perceptions of Christ were formed were varying representations of gentleness, healing, teaching, calming, reassuring, and suffering. The only instance of hostility I recall was Jesus' reaction to the money changers in the Temple. Basically, I was told that Christ is peace, and one day he would return to share it. Since then I have spent more time reading, studying scripture, and reexamining Jesus' return. Peace will come, but it will be found on the other side of a brutal battle.

In particular, two passages have completely changed my frame of reference for his return, and neither one is pleasant, peace-filled, or calming. The first is a passage from Matthew 10:34–39, in which Christ, states that he is not coming back with peace, but with a sword. He goes on to say that he will set men against their fathers and other relatives against one another; even in-laws are not immune. Literally, he says, "A man's foes shall be they of his own household." He is explaining that people will be divided, not as they are related as family or not, but by whether they believe in and follow Christ or not. Jesus is not interested in the depths of our love for our own parents, children, or relatives. He demands that his presence be our top relationship priority.

The second passage comes from several versus in the Book of Revelation (1:16, 2:16, and 19:15) where Christ's physical return is described. Specifically, these verses tell of a double-edged sword coming from his mouth, how he will smite the nations with it, and how his breath will kill the wicked. The Son of God does not need a weapon in order to kill anything or anyone, so I believe that the sword (with no dull side) is intended to represent "the Word of God." Jesus will show no mercy to those who do not honor and obey his Gospel. His words have always had tremendous power. Just as he commanded bodies to be healed and nature to yield to his authority, so will the future words from his mouth bring mankind to suffering and carnage far worse than simple death. He has provided man with his promise of salvation, but this covenant did not come without the ultimate sacrifice. For those who choose to ignore or defy his words and warnings, so shall they be judged and punished by them. Christ's coming back to take vengeance on the evildoers will be the furthest event from peaceful that you can imagine.

As a matter of fact, most of the scriptural passages I remember regarding Jesus' conversations with others seemed to stir things up and make people feel uncomfortable. He divided people, even within his own lifetime, into believers and nonbelievers. He pushed people's buttons and made them squirm in the presence of their own consciences and sinfulness. Peace will reign in Christ's kingdom, but that peace will only be found by those who are welcomed into his heavenly domain. For the rest of mankind, the opposite will be true. As Christians, we are called to pray for each other and for people who have not found Jesus in their hearts. Be diligent in following Christ's commands and extending his message to others. So when the time of his second coming is here, you will be comforted and protected in his merciful hands.

Focus for the Week

What are your personal beliefs about Christ's return? Are they based in scripture, what you've been taught, or opinions you have discussed with others? Do Jesus' words make you uncomfortable? Why? His reference to dividing families can be quite scary, especially since some of us consider those bonds to be the strongest and most intimate relationships we have. Take time to consider how his words affect your perspective on family and friendship ties. Do you put relatives before your faith? What can you do to find a way to put Jesus before everyone else in your life?

Passages

Matthew 10:34–39
Revelation 1:16, 2:16, 19:15

Are You Ready?

Indicators of Christ's impending return are popping up all over the globe as clearly as the lights on a dashboard. These signs are fulfilling biblical prophecies that count down to Jesus' appearance. Although many generations perceived that this event was shortly forthcoming, we have witnessed some very specific and startling events recently.

In the last ten to twenty years alone, the frequency of devastating fires, floods, and other natural disasters (hurricanes, typhoons, tsunamis, etc.) has increased and become more severe.

- Violence within and between nations is spiraling out of control.
- Civilization, especially in wealthier nations, is rapidly degrading in morals, values, common sense, and accountability of any kind.
- Political systems in the international community are breaking down and collapsing, and radical terrorist groups are killing indiscriminately while trying to buy their way into an afterlife that does not exist.
- The four seasons are no longer clearly defined by temperature, precipitation, foliage, or animal behavior.
- Christianity has become a prime target for anyone who does not believe in Jesus, and persecution of Christians is on the rise.
- The plans for the third Temple are complete and ready to go when the time arrives.
- The Succession of Pontiffs provides only one more pope to be appointed to service at the Vatican before Christ's return.
- More and more false prophets are coming forward with everything from self-proclamations of actually *being* Christ to "evidence" of Jesus' body being found

with those of his friends, family, and child, to new "Gospels" coming out of the woodwork, to those who claim to be healers, seers of the future, and whatever else they can conjure up for attention. Satan is generating as much propaganda as he can in order to mock, distract, and mislead those who might find their way to Christ.

- The most profound shift has been that approximately six million Muslims per year are now seeing visions or having dreams of Jesus and are converting to Christianity without hesitation. This information was revealed by Saudi cleric Sheikh Ahmad al Qataani during an interview for an Aljazeera broadcast in 2001.[4] Further comments indicated that the individuals who experienced these visions and dreams are coming forward from African, Middle Eastern, Asian, Western, and other countries around the world. Their demographics vary in sex, age, and level of education. Most risk execution for this conversion, since their culture's system of beliefs does not tolerate those who follow other faiths. Jesus is calling to them, even though their lives and "education" have done nothing but promote hate for him and his followers. The cleric wrapped up his comments on Christianity's spread by saying that it was a tragedy. So, are you ready?

We are now in a time when Christians must block out the evil and empty business of the devil and cling to scripture. Do not get caught up in anger, disbelief, and hype about our Lord. Stay the path of sharing the Gospel, living to do his will, keeping your heart and mind within his commandments, and asking for his forgiveness every day. Times will only become more hectic, emotionally unstable, and increasingly filled with conflict. The only aspect of the world we can control is our relationship with Christ. Are you ready to stick with the truth and let the lies, deception, and manipulation pass you by? Are you ready to let your armor of God cast off doubt and fear? Are you ready to be comfortable in your trust of the Lord, though the world may do its best to make you uncomfortable and miserable?

If you are, then the actual date of his second coming is irrelevant because you will persevere until that time. He will provide the strength and love you need to be sustained. His promise stands. Praise be to Christ—our Savior, protector, and friend.

Focus for the Week

Be aware of the misinformation that is being and will continue to be spread about Christ. Understand that God told us it would eventually come and use this knowledge to praise him and thank him for telling us in advance through the scriptures. Let every tidbit of false information energize you to pray even more diligently and read his book more thoroughly.

Passages

Acts 2:17–21
Mark 13:1–37

Observation

Christianity is not a religion. *Jesus encompasses the history, truth, and purpose of mankind's relationship with its creator.* He is infinite in power, wisdom, love, authority, and righteousness. Every aspect of life pales in comparison to his magnificence. Christianity is a state of faith, acceptance, humility, growth, thankfulness, love, and devotion. No label or designation suffices to embody our Savior. Simply, he is the *I Am*.

Afterword

I genuinely hope that sharing my experiences and faith will serve to affirm and encourage others who may be going through similar things. The publication of *Walking Faith Forward* was not intended for seeking approval or agreement, but I hope it will help to lift up those who need support and introspection into their own lives and faith. Rough days are inevitable, but we can trust that Jesus will see us through and will hear the prayers of all those who ask for his blessing on our behalf. Christ is everything we need. Continue to spread his word with confidence and enthusiasm.

References

Christmas Lore. "The History of the Yule Log." http://www.christmaslore.com/the_history_of_the_yule_log.html (accessed December 18, 2006).

Cinara, Paul. "Jesus Christ Saved a Fanatic Muslim—Testimony of Paul Cinara." *Salem Voice Ministries.* http://www.salemvoice.org/ciniraj.html (accessed March 19, 2007).

Holidays on the Net. "The History of Christmas." http://www.holidays.net/christmas/story.htm (accessed March 24, 2007).

Mitchell, Chris. "Visions of Jesus Stir Muslim Hearts." *CBN News,* February 20, 2007. http://www.cbn.com/CNBnews/69001.aspx (accessed March 22, 2007).

Olsen, Ted. "The Real Saint Nicholas." *ChristianityToday.com.* http://www.christianitytoday.com/history/newsletter/christmas/nick.html (accessed March 22, 2007).

Price, Dr. J. Randall. "Will There Be a Third Temple?" *Jewish Voice Today,* Jan./Feb. 2004. http://www.dunami.com/articles/Israel/third_temple_built.htm (accessed March 23, 2007).

Roberts, B. "Io Saturnalia!" 2001. http://www.members.aol.com/barbtail (accessed March 24, 2007).

Rosenberg, Joel C. "Israel: Plans for Third Jewish Temple Developing." *AfricanCrisis.org.* http://www.africancrisis.org/default2.asp (accessed March 23, 2007).

Sina, Ali. "Islam in Fast Demise." *FaithFreedom.org.*
http://www.faithfreedom.org/oped/sina31103.htm (accessed
March 24, 2007).

St. Nicholas Center—Discovering the Truth about Santa. "Bishop
of Myra." http://www.stnicholascenter.org/Brix?pageID=40
(accessed March 19, 2007).

St. Nicholas Center—Discovering the Truth about Santa. "Gift-
Giver." http://www.stnicholascenter.org/Brix?pageID=43
(accessed March 19, 2007).

St. Nicholas Center—Discovering the Truth about Santa. "Origin
of Santa." http://www.stnicholascenter.org/Brix?pageID=35
(accessed March 19, 2007).

St. Nicholas Center—Discovering the Truth about Santa. "Saint
in Bari." http://www.stnicholascenter.org/Brix?pageID=41
(accessed March 19, 2007).

Swank, Jr., J. Grant. "Muslims Turn to Christ." *The American
Daily,* January 2, 2007.
http://www.americandaily.com/article/17053 (accessed March 19,
2007).

10 Holidays. "Yule Log—Origins and Trivia."
http://www.thehistoryofchristmas.com/trivia/yulelog.htm
(accessed December 18, 2006).

"The Detective and the Toga: Festivals."
http://www.histmyst.org/festivals.html (accessed March 19,
2007).

Wikipedia. "Saint Nicholas."
http://www.en.wikipedia.org/wiki/Saint_Nicholas (accessed
March 22, 2007).

Wikipedia. "Saturnalia."
http://www.en.wikipedia.org/wiki/Saturnalia (accessed March 19, 2007).

Wikipedia. "Yule Log."
http://www.en.wikipedia.org/wiki/Yule_log (accessed March 19, 2007).

Endnotes

1. Roberts, B., "Io Saturnalia!" http://www.members.aol.com/barbtail.

2. "The Detective and the Toga: Festivals," http://www.histmyst.org/festivals.html.

3. Wikipedia, "Saturnalia," http://www.en.wikipedia.org/wiki/Saturnalia.

4. 10 Holidays, "Yule Log—Origins and Trivia," *The History of Christmas*, http://www.thehistoryofchristmas.com/trivia/yulelog.htm.

5. St. Nicholas Center—Discovering the Truth about Santa, "Bishop of Myra," http://www.stnicholascenter.org/Brix?pgID=40.

6. Swank, Jr., J. Grant, "Muslims Turn to Christ," *The American Daily*, http://www.americandaily.com/article/17053.

About the Author

Melanie Blievernicht currently resides in Woodstock, Georgia, where she works as a secretary. In addition to public speaking and her passion for writing, she enjoys reading, ministry work, tennis, horseback riding, camping, motorcycles, and activities around the water. She is also an avid animal lover with a soft spot in her heart for rescues.

Ms. Blievernicht may be contacted at
www.melanieblievernicht.com
or walkingfaithforward@yahoo.com

LaVergne, TN USA
05 May 2010
181503LV00002B/1/P